Lopes de Cabano

A New Practical and Easy Method of Learning the Portuguese Language

Salzwasser

Lopes de Cabano

A New Practical and Easy Method of Learning the Portuguese Language

1. Auflage | ISBN: 978-3-84605-006-4

Erscheinungsort: Frankfurt, Deutschland

Erscheinungsjahr: 2020

Salzwasser Verlag GmbH

FRANZ THIMM'S

SERIES

OF

EUROPEAN GRAMMARS

AFTER MEISSNER'S

EASY AND PRACTICAL METHOD.

PART V.

THE PORTUGUESE LANGUAGE.

LONDON:

FRANZ THIMM,

FOREIGN BOOKSELLER AND PUBLISHER.

24 BROOK STREET, GROSVENOR SQUARE W.

1869.

A NEW

PRACTICAL AND EASY METHOD

OF LEARNING THE

PORTUGUESE LANGUAGE.

BY

LOPES DE CABANO.

AFTER THE SYSTEM OF

Meissner.

Third Improved Edition.

LONDON:

FRANZ THIMM,

FOREIGN BOOKSELLER AND PUBLISHER.

24 BROOK STREET, GROSVENOR SQUARE W.

1869.

PREFACE.

Meissner's new and improved

System

of learning Foreign Languages.

The study of foreign languages having become general, the methods of teaching them have altered and improved, so as to unite the changes which philology has suggested, with those which the comparison of languages has taught.

The publisher has had this aim in view in the series of Foreign Grammars which has been issued under the title of

Franz Thimm's

Series of European Grammars

after Meissner's easy and improved method.

These grammars combine Theory with Practice, and follow the ideas which eminent men have adopted, as to the clearest and most rational method of teaching languages.

The celebrated philosopher *Leibnitz* remarked *"my opinion with regard to grammar is this, most is learned by use — the rules must be added for finish"*, and the learned philologist *Facciolati* observes *"I am indebted to the classical authors for every thing I know, to the grammarians I owe nothing."*

Seidenstücker was the first who in 1811 introduced this new Method for the Latin, Greek and French Languages, and to him belongs in justice the merit of having introduced a rational system of tuition. Ahn who made use of his method long after in 1834, acknowledges in his Preface, Seidenstücker as the originator of the System. There was however an essential point omitted even in these books, namely that

the grammatical form should *precede* the Exercises, so that the learner should at once be made acquainted with the grammatical structure of the foreign language, without which, he could never attain a thorough knowledge of it; this was first done in a masterly manner by Meissner in his German Grammar

and is the principle which has been followed in FRANZ THIMM's *Series of European Grammars* and which gives it a distinct feature of progress over the former systems pursued.

On these valuable principles the following grammars have been published:

for the German Language by	MEISSNER.
- - French	-	- AHN.
- - Italian	-	- MARCHETTI.
- - Spanish	-	- SALVO.
- - Portuguese	-	- CABANO.
- - Danish	-	- LUND.
- - Swedish	-	- LENSTRÖM.
- - Dutch	-	- AHN.
- - Hebrew	-	- HERXHEIMER.
- - Russian	-	- ALEXANDROW.
- - Latin	-	- SEIDENSTÜCKER.
- - Modern Greek		- VLACHOS.
- - Icelandic	-	- RASK.

The prevalent idea in these grammars is that of teaching a language easily and pleasantly, of adapting it to every capacity, of removing all unnecessary difficulties and at the same time of imparting the necessary grammatical knowledge.

In this respect therefore

Franz Thimm's Series of Grammars

is not only original, but extending the new Method to all the Languages of Europe it is unique.

The excellent Grammars by Bösche, Müller and Leisten have been made use of for this work.

INDEX.

Part II.

SECOND COURSE.

FIRST COURSE.

The Pronunciation.

1. The Alphabet.

The Portuguese Alphabet is composed of the 25 following letters:

	pronounced			pronounced
a	ah		*n*	ennay
b	bay		*o*	o
c	say		*p*	pay
d	day		*q*	kay
e	ai		*r*	erray
f	effay		*s*	essay
g	jay		*t*	tay
h	aghah		*u*	oo
i	ee		*v*	vay
j	dshod		*x*	shees
k	kah		*y*	ypsilon
l	ellay		*z*	zea.
m	emmay			

There are six vowels: *a, e, i, o, u* and *y*, the rest are consonants.

2. The Accent.

The Portuguese language has several accents:

the ´ acute accent,

the ^ circumflex accent, to pronounce the syllable long,

the ˜ hyphen, called *til*, is set over some letters as a substitute for *m*, as: *lã* for *lam* — *bẽ* for *bem* — *huã* for *huam.*

3. The Vowels.

A 1. is pronounced like the *a* in the English word p a t h, when it has the acute accent ´:

  chá, tea == *dá*, he gives — *lá*, there.

2. it is pronounced short and clear like the *a* in f a t h e r :

  capitão, the captain (first *a*),

or if found before the double consonants: *cc*, *ll*, *mm*, *nn*, *pp*, *ss*, *tt*, as:

  acclamar, to call out — *annullar*, to annul
  alludir, to allude — *appellar*, to appeal.

3. it has a soft and aspirated sound at the end of words if not accentuated: *vergonha*, the shame. If the hyphen ˜ *til* stands over the *a* it takes a nasal sound:

irmãa (pr. irmāng), the sister — *lã* (pr. lāng), the world.
irmão (pr. irmāon), the brother; *ang* and *on*, must be pronounced like the french, as: l'*ange*, patr*on*.

E has three sounds:

1. open but short like *ai* in the English word b a i l , or the german *ä*, when with the acute accent ´ as:

    pé, foot — *fé*, belief — *sé*, cathedral, the see

or in: *mel*, honey — *he*, he is

    quero (pr. kayro), 1 will,

and in the verbs ending in *er*:

  recebér (pr. ressaybayr), *conceder* (pr. conssaydayr),
      crescer (pr. cress-sàyr).

2. long, when with the circumflex ^ over it, like the german *e*, as:

    lé, he reads — *vé*, he sees — *rêde*, the net

3. It is almost mute at the end of words without the accent, as:

    liberdădĕ, liberty — *amizādĕ*, friendship.

1 is pronounced like *e* in the English word m e, and it is only the accent that determines the´ pronunciation, as:
    timido, *timoré*, — *difficil*, *javalí*,
long in the first, short in the second word.

O has three sounds:

1. clear and strong in: *mólho*, *do* (as in pōnd, bōnd).

2. soft and long as in English rōll, gore, more:
>   *bôlo*, cake — *gôrdo*, fat — *rapôsa*, the fox (fem.).

3. quite short, almost like *oo* in:
>>   *poder*, to be able — *molho*, a bundle

almost pronounced like *molyou*, *medo* (pr. maydoo).
at the end of words (like the english in *wood*).

U is pronounced like the *oo* in the word w o o d, but the pronunciation depends much upon the length of the syllables, as in *túmulo*, the grave, the first *u* is long, the second is short. If provided with the *til* ˜ and before *m* and *n* it takes the nasal sound.

>   If it follows after *g* and *q*, it is either aspirated, or it is quite mute, as: *guerra* (gerrah), war — *quero* (kayro), I will — *quieto* (key-eh-to), quiet. In *qual*, it is slightly sounded to distinguish it from the noun *cal*, the chalk.

Y is pronounced like the vowel *I*.

---

4. The Consonants.

B is pronounced like the English *B*.

C before *a, o, u, l* and *r* is pronounced like *k*, as:
>   *cavallo* (kahvallo), the horse — *cravo* (krahvo), the pink
>   *cuidado* (kooeedado), the care.

Before *e* and *i* it sounds like *s*, as:
>   *ceo* (sayo), heaven — *cigarro* (seegarro), cigar.

If the *c* before *a, o, u* has a cedilla (*ç*) it sounds like *ss*, as:
>   *caça* (kassah), chase — *aço* (asso), the steel
>   *açucar* (assookar), sugar.

The double *cc* is distinctly heard only before *e* and *i*, the first sounds like *k*, the second like *s*, as:
>>   *accidente* (akseedentay), the accident.

In most cases it sounds only like one *c*: *occidente* (pr. ossee-dentay).

D is pronounced like the English.

F is pronounced like the English.

before *a, o* and a consonant is pronounced like the English
g, as: *gordo,* fat — *gravo,* grave.

g before *e* and *i* sounds like the *j* in the English word
j o y, as: *general, genro* (like the french *jenro*),

gua almost sounds like the English *wa,* as: *guarda,* pr.
gwarda.

gue is pronounced gay.

gui is pronounced gee, as: *guerra* (gerrah), *guia* (geeah).

H is only softly aspirated in few words, as: *anhelar, hálito;*
otherwise it is mute, as:

homem (omem), man — *hora* (ora), hour.

Many writers drop the *h* at the beginning and write *um,
uma,* instead of: *hum, huma.*

J is pronounced like the English *j.*

K only occurs in foreign words and is pronounced like the
English *k.*

L is pronounced like the English *L.*

at the beginning of words, or between two vowels when
it belongs to the second syllable, is pronounced like the
English *m,* as: *menino,* child — *amar,* to love.

It takes a nasal sound at the end of words, or when
it follows after *a, e, i, o* or *u* which cannot well be de-
scribed, as: *condição,* condition — *bem* (bang), well —
bom (bong), good: the french nasal sound always gives
the proper pronunciation, *bom* (pr. bon), *tem* (pr. ten).

N is pronounced like the English *n,* but has the same pecu-
liarities as *m;* at the end always like the french *n*: *irman.
maçan.*

P is pronounced as in English.

Q sounds like *k,* as: *quero* (kayro), I will; *aqui* (pr. a-kee).

R is pronounced as in English.

S is pronounced as in English; between two vowels it sounds
like *z.*

T is pronounced like the English.

V do. do.

X has three sounds.

1. It sounds generally like *sh,* as:

xarope (sharope), syrup — *enxaqueca* (anshakeykah), headache.

2. After *e* it is pronounced like *ks*, as:
    extenção, extenuado, expulso, excellente.

3. Between two vowels it is pronounced like *gz*, as: *exactamente, exornar*, except in: *paixão, puxo, Alexandre, baixo*, and some other words, where it sounds like *sh*.
    The *x* must be pronounced so softly that it is scarcely audible.

Z sounds like the English, as: *zelo, zona.* — At the end of words it sounds like *s*, as: *rapaz, luz, voz.*

---

5. Double Consonants.

The Portuguese Language has the following double consonants:

Ch 1. is pronounced like the English *ch*, or the german *sch*, as:
    acho, chaga, marchar.

2. it is pronounced like *k* in words derived from Latin or Greek as:
    monarchia, archeo, archonte, Achilles.

Ct drops the *c* in the pronunciation: *acto* (ahto), *electrico* (elaytreekoo).

Lh is pronounced like the *ll* in the English word b i l l i a r d s or in the French words „fille, bouilli", as:
    mulher, woman — *mólho*, the bundle.

Mp sounds like *n*, as: *prompto* (pr. pronto), *assumpto* (aszoonto), in compounds it retains the *mp* sound.

Nh is pronounced like the French *gn* in „espagne, peigner", as: *ganho*, I win — *banho*, bath — *manha*, trick.

Ph is pronounced like *f*, as: *philosophia.*

Rh and **Th** are pronounced like *r* and *t*.

---

6. The Diphthongs.

The Portuguese Language has two kinds of diphthongs: the pure, those which are distinctly pronounced, and the nasal diphthongs, pronounced with a nasal sound.

Each vowel is pronounced by itself as: *áula* (pr. ah-oo-lah), *rêi* (ray-ee), *rio* (ree-o), *lagôa* (lago-ah), *heróe* (ayro-ay), *boi* (bo-ee), *sôa* (szo-ah), *ou* (o-oo), *eu fui* (ay-oo foo-ee).

Pure Diphthongs.

ae, as: *taes, olivaes.*
ai, (the *a* and *i* do not blend), as: *pai* (pa-ee), *ai* (a-ee),
ao,   as: *páo* (pá-o), *máo* (ma-o).
au,   — *aula, auto, paula, causa.*
ei, ey, — *rei, rey, lei, sei.*
éi,   — *papéis, réis.*
eo,   — *deo, mordeo, viveo.*
éo,   — *Céo, véo, réo.*
eu,   — *eu, euro, meu, seu.*
io,   — *pio, rio, vio, ouvio.*
oa,   — *loa, toa.*
oe,   — *heroe, dóe, róe.*
oi,   — *boi.*
ôo, oo,— *vôo, sôo, môo.*
ou,   — *ou, ouvir, douto.*
ui, uy, — *fui, Rui.*

In the above the first vowel is preeminent, in the following the second vowel has most emphasis.

ea, as: *lactea, área.*
eo, — *lacteo, arboreo.*
ia, — *gloria.*
oa (pron. *oá* and *oá*), as: *agoa, coadura, coalho.*
ui (pron. *uí*), as, *quirinal, inquirir.*
uo (pron. *uó*), as: *equoreo.*
uu (pron. *uú*), as: *equuleo.*

Nasal Diphthongs.

The til ˜ always gives to the final syllable the nasal sound of the french *n*, *allemã* (pr. alleyman), *allemão* (pr.
french

allaymon), *põe* (po-en), *sermões* (pr. sermo-ens), *aldeãos* (pr.
    french   french   french
aldaya-ons).
    french

ãa (bad or old orthography, better *am* or *an*), as: *maçãa* (mas-
                         sang), apple, *irmãa* (ir-mang), sister.
ãe (better *aem, aen*), as: *capitães* (kapeeta-engs), captains,
                      cães (ka-engs), dogs.
am, as: *amparo* (ang-paro), protection.
an, as: *andar* (ang-dar), to go.
ão (better orthogr. *aõ. am, an*), as: *capitão*, captain.
em, ẽe, ẽem, as: *lem* or *lẽem* (lay-eng), they read.
                 bem, good.
im, as: *fim* (fing), the end.
õe (*oem, oen*), as: *põe* (pong-eng), *nações* (nahs-so-engs).
om, as: *bom* (bong), good.
um, un, as: *mundo* (moong-do), the world.

The Portuguese have also syllables of three vowels, such, as:

eei, éio, eão, ião,

as: *eia*, hallo! — *meia*, half — *ideia*, idea — *rodeão*, they
surround — *vivião*, they lived.

Reading Lesson for the Pronunciation.

Manifesto é que, como entre todas as nações que
manee-festoo ay kay komo entray todas ass nasso-ens*) kay
no mundo ha, nenhuma se allongou tanto de
noo moon-doo ah, nenjoo-mah szeh allon-goh-oo tantoo day
sua terra natural como a nação portugueza, pois
szooah terrah natooral komo ah nasza-on portoogayzah po-is
sendo do ultimo occidente e derradeira parte
szendoo doo ultee-moo oszeedentay ay derrahday-ee-rah partay

---

*) the — under the letters denotes the french pronunciation.

do mundo onde (como Plinio diz) os elementos
doo moon-doo onday (komo Pleeneeo dee-ez) os elementos
da terra, agua e ar, fazem sua demarcação
dah terrah, ahgooah ay ahr, fas-en szooah daymar-kahszah-on
penetraram tudo o que o mar, oceano cerca, e
penetrahran toodoo o kay oh mahr oszayahnoo szerkah, ay
comsigo levaram sua lingua, a qual tão pura-
konszeego layvahran syooah lingooah, ah kwahl tahon poorah-
mente se falla em muitas cidades da Africa que
mentay szay fallah en moointas szeedahdes dah Afrikah kay
ao nosso jugo são sujeitas, como no nosso
ahoh noszo joogo szahon szoo-je-ee-tas komo no noszo
Portugal, e em muitas provincias da Ethiopia,
Portoogahl, ay en moo-intas prohvin-szee-ahs dah Aytheeo-pee-ah
da Pérsia e da India, onde temos cidades e
dah Părszee-ah ay dah Indeea, onday taymos szeedahdes ay
colonias, e nas muitas e grandes · ilhas do mar
kolonee-as ay nass moo-intas ay grandes eeljahs doo mahr
oceano. E a lingua portugueza se pode ter em
oszay-ah-no. ay ah lingooah portoogayzah szay poday tayr en
muito e chamar ditosa, pois por ella se
moo-into ay shahmahr deetoh-zah po-ees por ellah szay
annunciou e manifestou a tantas gentes, e
ahnnoon-szee-o-oo ay maneefestoh-oo ah tantas jayntes ay
de tão remotas e estranhas provincias, a fé de
day tahon raymotas ay estrahnjahs proveen-szee-ahs ah fay day
Nosso Senhor Jesus Christo, e foi causa de se
noszoh szenjhor Jesoos Kreesto ay fo-ee ka-oosah day szay
tirarem as erronias e trevas em que a mondo
tee-rah-ren ahs errohneeas ay trayvahsz en kay oh moon-doo
vivia.
vee-vee-ah.

Duarte Nunes do Leão.

Dotes peculiares da lingua portugueza. A lingua
Dotes paykoolee-ahres dah lingoo-ah portoo-gayzah ah lingoo-ah
portugueza, assim na sua suavidade da
portoo-gayzah, asseen nah szooah szoo-ah-vee-dah-day dah

pronunciação como na gravidade e com-
pro-noon-szeeah-szahon komoh nah grahveedahday ay com-

posição das palavras, é lingua excellente . . .
pozee-szahon dass pahlahvras ay lingoo-ah eggzaylentay

E' branda para deleitar, grave para encarecer,
ay brandah parah day-lay-ee-tahr grahvay parah enkahray-szayr,

efficaz para mover, dôce para pronunciar,
effee-kahsz parah mohvayr dohszay parah pronoon-szee-ahr

breve para resolver, e accommodada ás materias
brayvay parah rayzolvayr, ay akomohdahdah asz mahtayree-as

mais importantes da practica e escriptura. Para
mahis importantes dah pratteecah ay escreetoorah. Parah

fallar é engraçada com um modo senhoril. Para'
fallahr ay angrahszahdah kon oom modoo senjohreel. Parah

cantar é suave com um certo sentimento que
kantahr ay szooahvay kon oom szayrtoo szenteementoo kay

favorece a musica. Para pregar é substanci-
fahvorayszay ah mooseekah. Parah praygahr ay soobstanszee-

osa, com uma gravidade que auctorisa as sen-
ohsah kon oomah grahvee-dah-day kay aootoree-zah ahs szen-

tenças. Para escrever cartas, nem tem infinita copia
tenszahs. parah escrayvayr kartas nen ten infeeneetah kopee-ah

que damne, nem brevidade esteril que a limite,
kay dan-nay nen brayveedah–day estayreel kay ah lee-meetay

Para historias nem é tão flórida que se derrame,
parah ees-toree-as nen ay ta-on floreedah kay szay dayr-ramay

nem tão sécca que busque o favor das alheias.
nen tahon szaykah kay booskay oh fahvohr dahs aljay-ee-ahs

A pronunciação não obriga a ferir o
ah pronoon-szee-ah-szah-on nah-on obreegah ah fayreer oh

céo da bóca com aspereza, nem a arrancar as pa-
szay-oo dah bokah kon aspayrayzah nen ah arancar ahs pah-

lavras com vehemencia do gargalo. Escreve-se
lahvras kon vay-eh-men-szee-ah doo gargahloo escrayvay-szay

da maneira que se lé, e assim se falla. Tem
dah mahnay-ee-rah kay szay lay ay ahszin szay fallah. Ten

de todas as linguas o melhor: a pronunciação
day todas ahs lingoo-ahs oh meljohr ah pronoon-szee-ah-szahon

da latina: a origem da grega: a familiarida-
dah lateenah ah oreejen dah graygah ah famee-lee-ah-ree-dah-

de da castelhana: a brandura da franceza: a
day dah casteljah-nah ah brandoorah dah franszayzah ah

elegancia da italiana. Tem mais adagios e
aylayganszee-ah dah eetahlee-ahnah ten mahees adahjeeos ay

sentenças que todas as vulgares, em fé de sua
szenten-szahs kay todas ahs voolgahres en fay day szooah

antiguidade. E se á lingua hebrea, pela
ahntee-gee-dah-day ay szay ah lingoo-ah aybray-ah paylah

honestidade das palavras, chamaram sancta, certo
onestee-dah-day dass pahlavrass shahmahran szahntah szertoo

que não sei eu outra que tanto fuja das
kay nahon szayee ay-oo ootrah kay tahntoo foojah dass

palavras claras em materia descomposta quanto a
pahlavrass klahras en matayree-ah deskompostah kwantoh ah

nossa . . . . A lingua portugueza não desmerese
nossah ah lingooah portoo-gayzah nahon daysmayrayszay

lugar entre as melhores, para nella se escreverem
oogahr entray as meljhores parah naylah szay escrayvayren

materias levantadas, apraziveis, proveitosas, e
matayree-as layvantahdas ahprahscee-vay-ees provay-ee-tohsas ay

necessarias.
nayszays-sahree-ahs.   Francisco Rodrigues Lobo.

PART I.

1.

o, the (mas.)	*irmão*, brother
a, the (fem.)	*irmãa*, sister
pai, father	*e*, and
mãi, mother	*he*, is
bom (m.), *boa* (f.), good	

The Portuguese Language has but two genders, the masculine and feminine, the masc. article is *o*, the feminine article *a*.

Exercises.

O pai. A mãi. O irmão. A irmãa. O pai he bom, e a mãi he boa. O bom pai, a boa mãi. O bom irmão, a boa irmãa. O irmão he bom, a irmãa he boa.

2.

meu, minha, my — *alto*, great, tall — *pequeno*, little.

The sister is good. The father and the good brother. The good mother and the little sister. The tall brother. My brother is little. My little brother. My mother and my good sister. My father and my mother. My good mother and my little sister.

The adjective takes the gender and number of the substantive, it is placed, sometimes before, sometimes after, its substantive.

---

prudente, prudent	*alto,* high
triste, sad	*útil,* useful
o livro, the book	*doênte,* ill
a cása, the house	*é, he, está,* is

O pai prudente. A casa alta. O livro é util. A mãi está triste. O livro é util? Está o pai doente?

3.

Declension of the definite Article.

Masculine.

	Singular.		Plural.
Nom.	*o,* the		*os*
Gen.	*do,* of the		*dos*
Dat.	*ao,* to the		*aos*
Acc.	*o,* the		*os*
Abl.	*do,* from the		*dos*

Feminine.

	Singular.		Plural.
Nom.	*a,* the		*as*
Gen.	*da,* of the		*das*
Dat.	*á,* to the		*ás*
Acc.	*a,* the		*as*
Abl.	*da,* from the		*das*

Declension of the indefinite Article.

	Masculine.		Feminine.
Nom.	*um,* a		*uma*
Gen.	*de um,* of a		*de uma*
Dat.	*á um,* to a		*á uma*
Acc.	*um,* a		*uma*
Abl.	*de um,* from a		*de uma*

4.

Vocabulary.

moça, girl	*na (em a),* in the
bonito, pretty	*rua,* street
cavallo, horse	*garfo,* fork
agulha, needle	*estão,* are (from *estar*)
faca, knife	*nas (em as),* in, Acc.
leão, lion	*gaveta,* drawer
tigre, tiger	*tenho,* I have (from *ter*)
leopardo, leopard	*lido,* read (from *ler*)
são, are (from *ser*)	*isso,* this
animal, aes, animal	*nos (em os),* in, Acc.
feroz, wild	*livro,* book
estado, situation	*passeio,* I go
no (em o), in, Dat.	*pelo (por o),* through the
miseravel, miserable	*entrou,* he came in
em, in	*pela (por a),* through
que, which	*porta,* gate
elle, he	*boi,* ox
está, is (from *estar*)	*vaca,* cow
ella, she	

Exercises.

O pai he alto. A mãi he pequena. A moça he bonita. O cavallo do pai. A agulha da irmãa. A faca do irmão. O leão, o tigre e o leopardo são animaes ferozes. No estado miseravel em que elle está. Ella está na rua. O garfos estão nas gavetas. Tenho lido isso nos livros do C. Passeio pelo campo. Elle entrou pela porta. Um boi. Uma vaca.

5.

Vocabulary.

um (mas.) a	*a pênna*, the pen
úma (fem.) a	*a criánça*, the child
méu (mas.) my, mine	*o jardím*, the garden
minha (fem.) my, mine	*a cidáde*, the town
téu (mas.) thy, thine	*a árvore*, the tree
túa (fem.) thy, thine	*a mulhér*, the woman
séu (mas.) his	*o càvallo*, the horse
súa (fem.) her, hers	*grande*, tall, great, large
nósso (mas.) } our, ours	*pequèno*, little, small
nóssa (fem.) } our, ours	*ríco*, rich
vósso (mas.) } your, yours	*pobre*, poor
vóssa (fem.) } your, yours	

Um grande jardim. Minha rica mãi. Nosso grande tio. Sua penna é pequena? Seu cavallo é alto? Nossa mãi está doente. E' grande vossa cidade? Teu livro é util. E' prudente uma criança? Está doente sua mulher?

A good pen. My pen is good. A little horse. Your house is tall. His garden is large. Is your garden large? Her child is small. Her child is ill. It is a large town. Is your town rich? Our town is poor. The tree is large. Is it a large tree? The woman is poor. Is the woman ill?

6.

Vocabulary.

éste (m.) } this	*càda*, each, every
ésta (f.) } this	*nenhúm* (m.) } none
èsse (m.) } this one	*nenhúma* (f.) } none
éssa (f.) } this one	*não*, not
aquélle (m.) } that	*tambèm*, also
aquélla (f.) } that	*sèmpre*, always
qual, which	*núnca*, never

mas, but
conténte, content
o filho, the son
a filha, the daughter
o tío, the uncle

a tía, the aunt
o vizinho, the neighbour
o hómem, the man
o amígo, the friend

Aquelle jardim não é grande. Qual filha não está contente? Esse homem tambem está rico. Nenhuma criança é prudente. Não é cada livro util? Este homem está sempre contente; mas aquelle nunca. Qual é o teu amigo?

This is my son, and that is her daughter. That is his daughter and this is her son. Our friend is rich, but our neighbour is poor. He is also rich. Which sister is ill? Each pen is good. Which aunt is not rich? Is your uncle not rich? Is this neighbour always ill? My friend is never ill, but his wife is always ill. Is this man contented? or is he not contented?

7.

eu ténho, I have
elle, ella, tém, he, she, it has

nos témos, we have
elles, ellas tém, they have

---

a flór, the flower
a janélla, the window
o chapéo, the hat
o relógio, the watch
a fáca, the knife
a cárta, the letter
móço, nóvo, young, new
vélho, old

fórte, strong
applicádo, industrious
preguiçóso, lazy
boníto, pretty
já, already
aínda, yet
múito, very

Tem ella a nossa faca grande? Eu não tenho nenhuma flor. Elle tem um bonito chapeo. Seu tio tem um cavallo forte? Não tem elle uma carta? Aquella nova casa não tem janellas? Já tém ellas um relogio? Que discipulo applicado

não tem um livro novo? Tem elles um irmão preguiçoso?
Ainda não temos jardim.

———————

I have a pretty flower. Has she not already a hat? He
has a very good watch. We have no friend. That man has
a very young horse. The window is pretty. His hat is very
old. I have a strong knife. Has he not already my letter? I
have not yet had your letter.

———————

8.

Eu sóu or *eu estoû*, I am	*Nos somos* or *estamos*, we are
tu és or *tu estás*, thou art	*vos sóis* or *estáis*, you are
élle, élla é and *está*, he, she, it is	*élles, éllas são* and *estão*, they are

aqui, here; *hóje*, to day; *não*, no.

———————

The Portuguese like the Spaniards politely address the person to whom they speak as
1. Vóssa Mercê, written: *Vm.*; it means your grace,
   honour, worship. Sir, you etc. or
2. in a still higher form: Vóssa Senhoría or
3. without any pronoun in the third person

     as: *tém livros?* have you any books?
      está doente? are you ill?

———————

Nosso filho não está aqui hoje. Ellas não estão ricas.
Não é elle um preguiçoso? Tua faca já não é nova. Nós
tambem somos prudentes. Ainda não estais contentes? Vm.
já é homem.

———————

I am very unwell to-day. Thou art here? Is not this
your garden? No, it is not my garden, but that is my house.
She is very poor. We are very rich but not contented.
They are always very industrious. Are you already here? you
are not very prudent, my friend. Are they still here?

———————

9.

Vocabulary.

noticia, the news	*açor,* hawk
muito, very	*ave de rapina,* bird of prey
nobre, noble	*ignorancia,* ignorance
cão, dog	*erro,* error
ladrão, bark	*superstição,* superstition
rosa, rose	*deixei,* I left behind (deixar)
mais bello, more beautiful	*tia,* aunt
do que, than	*cama,* bed
tulipa, tulip	*menino, criança,* child, baby
verão, summer	*o braço,* the arm
quente, hot	*carta,* letter
inverno, winter	*mão,* hand
rigoroso, severe	*secretario,* secretary.
passaro, bird	*saltar,* to jump
cantão, sing (cantar)	*janella,* window
aguia, eagle	

The news is good. The horse is a very noble animal.
The dogs bark. The roses are more beautiful than the tulips.
The summers are hot and the winters severe. The birds sing.
The eagle and the hawk are birds of prey. Ignorance is the
mother of error, of superstition, and of prejudice. I left my
hat in the carriage. The aunt is in bed. She had her child
in her arms. He gave the letter into the hands of the secretary.
He jumped out of (*pela*) the window. I see a man and a
woman. A garden and a house.

Contractions of the Article with the Prepositions.

The Portuguese contract the article and preposition in
the following way:

from	*de o*	is formed	*do*			from	*em o*	is formed	*no*	
-	*de a*	-	-	*da*		-	*em a*	-	-	*na*
-	*de os*	-	-	*dos*		-	*em os*	-	-	*nos*
-	*de as*	-	-	*das*		-	*em as*	-	-	*nas*
-	*a o*	-	-	*ao*		-	*por o*	-	-	*pelo*
-	*a a*	-	-	*à*		-	*par a*	-	-	*pela*
-	*a os*	-	-	*aos*		-	*por os*	-	-	*pelos*
-	*a as*	-	-	*às*		-	*por as*	-	-	*pelas*

10.

On the Gender.

Masculine

are the names of all masculine persons, animals, and the occupations of men.

Vocabulury.

Imperador, Emperor	*foi,* was
foi, was (from *ser*)	*Frederico,* Frederick
morto, killed	*ambicioso,* ambitious
rei, king	*ferreiro,* the smith
chegou, he arrived	*diligente,* diligent
hontem, yesterday	*alfaiate,* tailor
jesuita, the Jesuit	*preguiçoso,* lazy
forão, they were	*gordo,* fat
expulsado, expelled	*gallo,* the cock
homem, man	*mais forte,* stronger
não ama senão, only loves	*de que,* than
a si mesmo, himself	*gallinha,* hen
Carlos, Charles	

O Imperador Paulo foi morto. El-Rei chegou hontem. Os jesuitas forão expulsados. O homem não ama senão a si mesmo. Carlos foi grande e Frederico ambicioso. O ferreiro he diligente e o alfaiate preguiçoso. O boi he muito gordo. O leão he muito feroz. O gallo he mais forte do que a gallinha.

11.

Vocabulary.

duque, duke	*morreo,* died
proclamado, proclaimed	*marcineiro,* the joiner
principe herdeiro, hereditary prince	*carpinteiro,* the carpenter
	trabalhão, they work

Luiz, Lewis	*marido* } *esposo* } husband
Henrique, Henry	*doente*, ill
poderoso, powerful	*tio*, uncle
touro, the bull	*sahio* (*sahir*), went out
matado, killed	*avó*, grandfather
vigilante, watchful	*primo*, cousin
bello, *formoso*, beautiful	*filho*, son
sanguinario *sanguinoso* *sanguinolento* } bloodthirsty	*dão*, (dar) they take
	passeio, walk.

The Duke of Braganza was proclaimed king. The hereditary prince died. The joiner and the carpenter work. Lewis was brave, and Henry powerful. The bull was killed. The watchful dog. The beautiful horse. The tiger is very bloodthirsty. The husband of this woman is very ill. The uncle went out. The grandfather, the father, the cousin and the son took a walk.

12.

Feminine Substantive.

The names of all feminine persons, animals and the occupations of women are feminine.

Vocabulary.

Imperatriz, empress	*avó*, grandmother
Rainha, queen	*neta*, granddaughter
estavão, they were	*jardim*, garden
igreja, church	*rapariga*, little girl
duqueza, duchess	*feia*, ugly
banho, bath	*mulher*, woman
alfaiata, sempstress	*obsequioso*, polite, good
concerta, (concertar) mends	*vaca*, cow
vestido, dress	*dá*, gives (from *dar*)
filha, daughter	*ite*, milk
tia, aunt	*chocando*, (chocar) hatching.

A Imperatriz e a rainha estavão na igreja. A duqueza está no banho. A alfaiata concerta um vestido. A mãi e a filha, a tia e a prima, a avó e a neta estão no jardim. A rapariga não he feia. A mulher he muito obsequiosa. A vaca dá leite. A gallinha está chocando.

13.

Vocabulary.

abbadessa, abbess
fallou, spoke (from *fallar*)
freira
religiosa } nun
sôr
mosteiro
convento } convent
princeza, princess
estar para, to be on the point
partir, to depart
condeça, the countess
casa, house
costureira, needlewoman
pespontar, to hem
lenço, de pescoço, neckhand-kerchief
esposa, the wife
negociante, merchant
muitas vezes, frequently
caprichoso, capricious
criada, the maid servant
varre, está varrendo, sweeps
cozinha, kitchen
cabra, goat
animal domestico, domestic animal

gata, cat
está brincando, plays
com, with
cachorra, young dog
minha, my, fem.
prima, cousin, fem.
irmãa, sister
theatro, theatre
leoa, lioness
juba, the mane
esta, this
egoa, mare
mais bello, more beautiful
cavallo capado, the stallion
Maria, Mary
não he tão, is not so
come, as
Marianna, Maryann
Inglaterra, England
sabio, wise
soberana, sovereign, f.
cozinheira, cook
mercado, market
diligente, diligent.

The abbess spoke with the nuns of the convent. The princess was on the point of departing. The countess was not at home. The needlewoman hems my pockethandkerchief. The wife of the merchant. The women are often very capricious. The servant sweeps the kitchen. The goat is a domestic animal. The cat plays with the young female dog. My cousin (*fem.*) and my sister were at the theatre. The lioness has no mane. This mare is more beautiful than that stallion. Mary is not so diligent as Maryann. Elisabeth of England was a wise sovereign. The cook went to market.

In Portuguese some of the names of animals are occasionally masculine and feminine; to denote the gender the words *macho*, male, or *femea*, female, are used, as:

     elephante macho, the male elephant,
     elephante femea, the female elephant.

Those substantives ending in *a* and *ãa* are feminine.

14.

Exercises.

Esta casa [1] tem uma boa [2] apparencia [3]. A rosa [4] he muito bella. A boca [5], a orelha [6], a cabeça [7], a testa [8] e a barba [9] são partes [10] do corpo [11] humano [12]. A janella [13] está aberta [14]. Esta agulha [15] he fina de mais [16]. Esta tinta não presta para nada. Quero aparar [17] uma penna [18]. Tenho [19] que escrever [20] uma carta [21]. Faça-me o favor [22] de me emprestar [23] uma folha de papel [24]. A garrafa [25] está na mesa [26]. Esta cerejeira [27] carrega [28] muito. Esta uva [29] está madura [30]. Esta vinha [31] está em optima [32] exposição [33].

1 house. 2 good. 3 appearance. 4 rose. 5 mouth. 6 ear. 7 head. 8 forehead. 9 chin. 10 part. 11 body. 12 human. 13 window. 14 open. 15 needle. 16 is too fine. 17 mend. 18 pen. 19 I have. 20 to write. 21 letter. 22 do me the favour. 23 lend. 24 sheet of paper. 25 bottle. 26 table. 27 cherry tree. 28 bears. 29 grape. 30 ripe. 31 vine. 32 the best. 33 situation.

The butter [1] is fresh [2]. With your permission [3]. The cup [4] is not washed [5]. I have the honour [6]. The beer [7] is excellent [8]. The oyster [9] is fresh. Bring me [10] a wafer [11]. — We have a beautiful [12] morning [13]. The door [14] is locked [15]. Spring [1] is the most agreeable [17] time of the year [18]. The harvest [19] will be [20] abundant [21].

1 manteiga. 2 fresco. 3 licença. 4 chicara. 5 lavado. 6 honra.
7 cerveja. 8 excellente. 9 ostra. 10 traga-me. 11 obrea.
12 lindo. 13 manhãa. 14 porta. 15 fechado. 16 primavera.
17 a mais agradavel. 18 estação. 19 colheita. 20 ha de ser.
21 abundante.

Exceptions.

The following substantives ending in *a* are masculine:

o aroma, the aroma	*o drama,* the drama
o axioma, the principle	*o mappa,* the map
o chá, the tea	*o idioma,* the idiom
o clima, the climate	*o planeta,* the planet
o cometa, the comet	*o poema,* the poem
o dia, the day	*o thema,* the theme.
o diadema, the diadem	

The nouns ending in *e*, are generally masculine, except:

1. those ending in *ade*, as: *verdade*, truth etc.,
2. those ending in *ie* or *ice*, as: *a velhice*, the age,
3. those ending in accented *é*, as: *a cheminé*, a chimney.

Nouns ending in *i, y, o, u* as well as those ending in *l, m, r, s* and *z* are with few exceptions all masculine.

Those ending in * õo*, are both masculine and feminine.

15.

Formation of the Plural.

Nouns ending in *a, e, i, y, o, u* and *ãa* form their plural by adding an *s* to the singular. As: *a rosa, as rosas; a arte, as artes; o filho, os filhos.*

Examples.

As rosas são mais bellas que as tulipas. Os rios correm[1] por terras despovoadas[2]. As arvores são muito frondosas[3]. As villas são ornadas[4] de duas igrejas. Eu não vi os pentes[5]. Os habitantes[6] destas comarcas[7] são Indios[8]. Elles tem maçãas. Novos Reis, novas leis. Deixei os bahús nos coches. Os ribeiros[9], algumas lagôas[10] e mesmo certos rios ficão em secco[11].

1 flow. 2 depopulated. 3 foliage. 4 ornamented. 5 comb. 6 inhabitants. 7 district. 8 Indian. 9 brook. 10 lake. 11 dry out.

These houses please me more than those edifices[1]. The villages[2] and towns in this district[3] are not very numerous[4]. The oxen[5], cows, goats, sheep[6] and cats[7] are domestic animals. There are[8] many wild boars[9], deer[10] and hares[11] in these forests[12]. The cranes[13] and storks[14] are birds of passage[15]. The huts[16] are made[17] of the trunks of trees[18].

1 edificio. 2 aldêa. 3 região. 4 numeroso. 5 boi. 6 ovelha. 7 gato. 8 ha. 9 javali. 10 veado. 11 lebre. 12 bosque. 13 grou. 14 cegonha. 15 ave de arribação. 16 barraca. 17 feito. 18 tronco d'arvore.

16.

Substantives ending in *ão*, form their plural in *ões*, as: *a condição*, condition, *as condições*.

Exceptions are:

> *Allemão*, the German, *Allemães*
> *Catalão*, the Catalonian, *Catalães*
> *cão*, dog, *cães* — *pão*, bread, *pães*
> *capitão*, captain, *capitães* — *tabellião*, notary, *tabelliães*.

The following only add an *s* in the Plural:

aldeão, the peasant	*a benção*, the blessing
anão, the dwarf	*christão*, Christ
ancião, the age	*cortezão*, the courtier

grão,	the corn		*orgão,*	the organ
irmão,	the brother		*pagão,*	the heathen
mão,	the hand		*rabão,*	the radish
orfão,	the orphan		*villão,*	the villain.

17.

Examples.

Elle abrio [1] communições entre as cidades e os sertões [2]. Os serões [3] são cumpridos. O districto he proprio [4] para todas as producções agricolas [5]. As terras são plantadas [6] e semeadas [7] de feijões [8] e melões [9]. Os Allemães fizerão [10] muitas invenções [11] uteis [12]. Os capitães não querem obedecer [13] ao general. Aqui [14] estão tres pães [15]. Os Cortezãos lisonjão [16] ao principe [17]. Os primeiros orgãos forão construidos [18] por um Allemão em 1312. Eis aqui [19] os dous [20] villãos. As casas são ornadas de balcões [21] de ferro. Aos orphãos manda-se [22] aprender [23] um olficio [24].

1 open. 2 the interior of the country. 3 evening. 4 is suitable. 5 agricultural produce. 6 planted. 7 sowed. 8 black bean. 9 melon. 10 make. 11 invention. 12 useful. 13 obey. 14 here. 15 bread. 16 flatter. 17 the prince. 18 constructed. 19 here are. 20 two. 21 balcony. 22 one lets. 23 learn. 24 a handicraft.

The passions [1] of women are often very violent [2]. The navigation [3] extended [4], at the beginning [5], only along the coast. Many revolutions [6] have broken out [7] in Europe in recent times [8]. The conditions [9] were rejected [10]. These places [11] are situated in the interior of the country [12]. The hunters [13] took [14] the dogs to the chase [15]. The Catalonians inhabit an important [16] province of Spain [17]. The notaries [18] protest [19] the bills of exchange [20]. His brothers were not at home [21]. The first

1 paixão. 2 violento. 3 navegação. 4 estender. 5 no principio 6 revolução. 7 rebentar. 8 no ultimo tempo. 9 condição 10 rejeitar. 11 povoação. 12 no interior do paiz. 13 caçador 14 levar. 15 caça. 16 consideravel. 17 Hespanha. 18 tabellião. 19 protestar. 20 lettra de cambio. 21 em casa.

Christians were much persecuted [22]. The heathens are still very numerous [23]. The radishes are very dear.

22 perseguir. 23 numeróso.

18.

Substantives ending in:

al, ol, ul change *l* into *es*, as: *a sinal*, a signal, *as sinaes*
el change *l* into *is*, as: *annel*, a ring, *anneis*
il change *l* into *s*, as: *o funil*, a funnel, *os funis*.

Examples.

conter, contain	*muitas vezes*, frequently
sal, salt	
mandar, to order	*o funil*, the funnel
furriel, lieutenant	*ao pé*, with
amizade, friendship	*barril*, the barrel
encontrar, to meet	*mandou*, had (let)
primavera, spring	*pór*, erect
terrestre, earthly	*pharol*, lighthouse.

As aguas contem differentes saes. Os animaes domesticos. Os generaes mandavão aos furrieis. Os coroneis estavão no conselho de guerra. Os varios sinaes de sua amizade. Não se encontra muitos caracoes nesta primavera. Os males terrestres são muitas vezes quasi insupportaveis. Os papeis estão na mesa. Os funis estão ao pé dos barris. O imperador mandou pór pharoes.

19.

The poignards [1] are ground [2]. These fishing rods [3] are good for nothing [4]. The goldsmith brought the rings [5]. The painter [6] has many brushes. Three consuls governed [7] France in 1803. The barrels [8] are full [9]. The officers [10] were very

1 punhal. 2 amolar. 3 o anzol. 4 não valem nada. 5 annel. 6 pintor. 7 governar. 8 barril. 9 cheio. 10 official.

much dissatisfied [11]. There are [12] different chalks [13]. I like [14]
pies [15]. — They will discover [16] your tricks [17].

11 descontente. 12 ha. 13 cal. 14 eu gosto. 15 pastel. 16 descubrir.
    17 ardil.

20.

Substantives ending in *m*, change their plural into *ns*, as:
bem, the treasure, *bens* — *viagem*, the journey, *viagens*.

Those ending in *r*, *s* and *z*, add *es* to the singular, as:
a colher, the spoon, *as colheres* — *ar*, the air, *ares*
deos, a God, *deoses* — *perdiz*, the partridge, *perdizes*;
    except:
ourives, the goldsmith, *ourives* — *caliz*, the chalice, *calices*
alferes, the ensign, *alferes*.

Examples.

As margens [1] verdejão [2] com a relva [3] dos prados [4]. Elle
fez [5] muitas viagens. Elle possue [6] muitos bens de raiz [7] na
cidade e fóra della [8]. Todos os homens são mortaes [9]. Os
sons dos instrumentos musicos. Os jejuns [10] não engordão [11].
O ceo [12] se cobre [13] de nuvens [14]. Os moradores [15] commer-
cião [16] em [17] madeiras de construcção [18]. Comprei [19] duas colheres de prata. As Imperatrizes de Russia e d'Austria chegárão [20]. Atire [21] a esse bando [22] de perdizes. Os Deoses se
ajuntão [23] no Olympo. Quasi [24] todos os freguezes [25] são Indios. Ha quatro calices na igreja. Os piratas [26] infestavão
os mares.

1 bank. 2 green. 3 turf. 4 meadow. 5 made. 6 possess. 7
(landed) property. 8 out of it. 9 mortal. 10 fasting. 11 to
make fat. 12 sky. 13 covered. 14 cloud. 15 inhabitants. 16
deal. 17 with. 18 timber. 19 to buy. 20 to arrive. 21 short.
22 flock. 23 assemble. 24 almost. 25 customer. 26 pirates.

21.

I hear [1] sounds [2]. The sun [3] hides [4] itself behind [5] thick [6]
clouds [7]. We have four ducks [8]. The passages [9] are locked [10].
The pictures [11] of Saints in this church are very numerous.

Our baggage[12] is still in the vessel. I offer[13] you my congratulations[14]. The air (*pl.*) is always[15] pure[16] in this country. I have eaten[17] four[18] quails[19]. He showed[20] me the scars[21] of his wounds[22]. In a battalion[23] there are eight ensigns. The goldsmiths came together. The chalices of the flowers. I was many times[24] in your house. The belligerent[25] powers.

1 ouvir. 2 tom. 3 sol. 4 esconder. 5 de. 6 grosso. 7 nuvem. 8 pato. 9 passagem. 10 fechar. 11 imagem. 12 bagagem. 13 dar. 14 parabem. 15 sempre. 16 puro. 17 comido. 18 quatro. 19 codorniz. 20 mostrar. 21 cicatriz. 22 ferida. 23 batalhão. 24 vez. 25 belligerante.

22.

Declension of Substantives.

Singular.

	Masculine.		Feminine.	
Nom.	*o homem,*	the man	*a mulher,*	the woman
Gen.	*do homem,*	of the man	*da mulher,*	of the woman
Dat.	*ao homem,*	to the man	*á mulher,*	to the woman
Acc.	*o homem,*	the man	*a mulher,*	the woman
Abl.	*do homem,*	from the man.	*da mulher,*	from the woman

Plural.

Nom.	*os homens,*	the men	*as mulheres*	the women
Gen.	*dos homens,*	of the men	*das mulheres,*	of the women
Dat.	*aos homens,*	to the men	*ás mulheres,*	to the women
Acc.	*os homens,*	the men	*as mulheres,*	the women
Abl.	*dos homens,*	from the men.	*das mulheres,*	from the women.

Nom.	*Deos,*	God	*Deoses,*	Gods
Gen.	*de Deos,*	of God.	*de Deoses,*	of Gods
Dat.	*a Deos,*	to God.	*a Deoses,*	to God
Acc.	*(a) Deos,*	God	*(a) Deoses,*	Gods
Abl.	*de Deos,*	from God.	*de Deoses,*	from Gods.

23.

Examples.

chapéo, the hat	*igualar*, to compare
offerecer, to offer	*deo*, gave (from *dar*)
batalha, the battle	*grande*, sound, great
inimigo, enemy	*bofetada*, box on the
jardim, garden	ear
luva, glove	*calçado*, paved
conde, Count	*fizerão*, they made
deixar, to leave	*cruel*, cruel
mordomo, steward	*guerra*, war
adular, to flatter	*comprar*, to buy
lisongeiro, the flat-	*livro*, book
terer	*livreiro*, bookseller
de sorte, in such a	*rancor*, the rancor,
manner	enmity.

O pai não está em casa. O chapéo do irmão. O general offereceo batalha ao inimigo. A mai ama a seu filho. A irmãa está no jardim. As luvas da mãi. O conde nada deixou ao seu mordomo. Adulando um lisongeiro ao Imperador Sigismundo, de sorte que o igualava a Deos, o Imperador deo ao lisongeiro uma grande bofetada. As ruas são calçadas. Os Portuguezes fizerão cruel guerra aos Indios. A mulher comprou o livro do livreiro. O rancor dos Francezes contra os Inglezes.

24.

Exercises.

The father loves [1] his daughter [2]. Mary loves her friend [3] (*fem.*). The eyes of Caroline equal [4] two [5] stars [6]. He gave the money to the woman, and paid the tailor [7] at the same time [8]. Two streams [9] of the province are designated [10] by this name [11]. Various estates [12] are touched [13] by this river. These offers [14] have been made to the colonists [15]. He delivered [16] the letter [17] to the secretary [18]. The Madeira is the *most important* [19] *tributary* [20] of the Amazon river [21]. The name of the Islands. The town is situated [22] on the left bank [23] of the river. The harbour [24] of Rio de Janeiro is the most beautiful ornament [25] of the city.

> 1 amar. 2 filha. 3 amiga. 4 igualar. 5 dous (*fem.* duas). 6 estrella. 7 alfaiate. 8 ao mesmo tempo. 9 ribeiro. 10 assignar. 11 nome. 12 fazenda. 13 regar. 14 offerecimento. 15 colono. 16 entregar. 17 carta. 18 secretario. 19 cabal, importante. 20 tributario. 21 rio do Amazonas. 22 jazer. 23 na margem esquerda. 24 porto. 25 ornato.

25.

On the Augmentatives and Diminutives.

The Portuguese language has the peculiarity of the Italian and Spanish languages in making Substantives and Adjectives, by the addition of a syllable augmentative or diminutive.

I. Augmentativos.

homem, a man — *homemzarão*, a large, powerful man
tolo, a fool — *toleirão*, a great fool
mulher, the woman — *mulherona*, a large masculine woman
tola, the foolish woman — *toleirona*, a very foolish woman.

II. Diminutivos.

are formed by changing the final vowel into *inho* or *inha*

casa, the house — *casinha*, a pretty little house
homem, a man — *homemzinho*, a little man
bicho, a worm — *bichinho*, a little worm
coitado, a poor man — *coitadinho*, a poor little fellow
bonito, pretty — *bonitinho*, rather pretty;

others are formed by adding: *zinho, zinha* or *sinho, inha*, as:

coração, the heart — *coraçãozinho*, dear little heart
cão, the dog — *cãozinho*, pretty little dog
irmão, the brother — *irmãozinho*, dear little brother
cabeça, the head — *cabeçinha*, pretty little head
mão, the hand — *mãozinha*, pretty little hand.

26.

The Adjective.

The Adjectives in Portuguese agree with the Substantives in gender and number.

1. Adjectives ending in *e*, *l* and *z*, remain unchanged in the feminine, as: *forte*, strong; *grande*, great; *cruel*, cruel; *amavel*, amiable.

2. Adjectives ending in *o* change the feminine into *a*, as: *o bonito*, the pretty, *a bonita*.

3. Those ending in *ú*, *m* and *r*, add an *a* in the feminine, as: *crú*, raw, *crúa* — *nú*, nude, *núa*

    um, a, *uma* — *nenhum*, none, *nenhuma*
    traidor, traitorous, *traidora* — *protector*, *protectora*.

4. Adjectives ending in *ão* change to *ãa* in the feminine, as: *luçáo*, brilliant, *luçãa* — *são*, healthy, *sãa*.

27.

The Plurals of Adjectives

are formed in the same manner as the plural of Nouns, as:

Singular.			Plural.	
Masc.		Fem.	Masc.	Fem.
forte,	strong,	*forte*	*fortes,*	*fortes*
gordo,	fat,	*gorda*	*gordos,*	*gordas*
crú,	raw,	*crua*	*crús,*	*cruas*
são,	healthy,	*sãa*	*sãos,*	*sãas* ·
igual,	equal,	*igual*	*iguaes,*	*iguaes*
amavel,	amiable,	*amavel*	*amaveis,*	*amaveis*
civil,	civil,	*civil*	*civis,*	*civis*
algum,	any one,	*alguma*	*alguns,*	*algumas*
protector,	protected,	*protectora*	*protectores,*	*protectoras*
capaz,	capable,	*capaz*	*capazes,*	*capazes.*

Observations.

1. The following add *s* to the plural:

meão, mediocre — *temporão*, timely
são, healthy — *villão*, bad.

2. The following change *il* into *eis* in the plural, as:

agil, swift — *aquatil*, aquatic — *debil*, weak
difficil, difficult — *docil*, docile — *ductil*, pliant
esteril, sterile — *facil*, easy — *fertil*, fertile
fossil, fossil — *fragil*, fragile — *futil*, futile
habil, clever — *ignobil*, disgraceful — *immobil*, immo-
veable.
indocil, stupid — *inhabil*, awkward — *inutil*, useless
inverosimil, unlikely — *portatil*, portable — *reptil*, reptile
util, useful — *verosimil*, probable — *versatil*, changeable
volatil, volatile — *volubil*, voluble.

3. *Simplez*, single, forms its plural in *simplez* and *simplices*.

28.

Examples.

A rua principal. As ruas principaes são calçadas. A igreja nova. A nova igreja. O homem velho [1]. A mulher velha. Os Indios atemorisados [2]. As mulheres Indias. A bella e grande cidade. O sobrinho [3] moribundo [4]. A victoria gloriosa. Este homem he mui villão e aquella mulher mui villãa. As mulheres são amaveis, os homens mui crueis. Um moço nú e uma criança nua. O homem he affavel e a mulher he tambem affavel. O genio contraditor e a observação contraditora. A filha he gorda e o filho he gordo. Os homens estão sãos e as mulheres sãas. O povo tranquillo e soffredor [5]. A sombria raiva [6] do Philippe. Os velhos bandos hespanhões [7]. Algumas [8] embarcações [9] que tinhão servido de piquetes [10]. Uma satisfacção inexplicavel. A igreja he uma das mais bellas do reino [11]. As aguas mineraes. O termino he fertil. O filho unico. A religião christãa. Um cavalheiro [12] christão [13]. A igreja de Santo Antonio he dedicada ao santo do seu nome. A margem [14] direita. A guarda [15] nacional.

O sobredito[16] districto. As grandes plantações[17] de cannas[18]. A pequena[19] aldêa[20]. Santos he uma cidade maritima a mercantil. As autoridades militares e civis. O rio aurifero.

1 old. 2 frightened. 3 nephew. 4 dying. 5 suffering. 6 hatred. 7 spanish. 8 some. 9 vessel. 10 watch. 11 reign. 12 knight. 13 christian. 14 shore. 15 the guard. 16 above named. 17 plantations. 18 sugar. 19 little. 20 village.

29.

Exercises.

The rich[1] man and the poor[2] woman. The pretty house. The large church[3]. The fertile fields[4]. The shoemaker is very industrious. The leafy[5] trees[6]. The wounded[7] soldier[8]. The beautiful bridges[9]. The numerous[10] products. The old uncle[11] and the fat aunt[12]. The horses are very handsome. The day is very bright[13]. The climate is very agreeable[14]. The winter[15] in Siberia[16] is very rigorous[17]. The geographical[18] and historical[19] Institute[20]. The tall man and the little woman. The above named[21] royal decree[22]. The generous[23] feelings[24]. The enormous[25] forests[26]. Some[27] somber and broad[28] rivers. The only[29] ornament. The warlike[30] Indians. The preceding[31] article[32]. The sea is very rough[33]. The following[34] day. The following days. He is silent[35] and grave[3]. The deep[37] love[38].

1 rico. 2 pobre. 3 igreja. 4 campo. 5 frondoso. 6 arvore. 7 ferido. 8 soldado. 9 ponte. 10 numeroso. 11 tio. 12 tia. 13 claro. 14 agradavel. 15 inverno. 16 Sibiria. 17 rigoroso. 18 geographico. 19 historico. 20 instituto. 21 mencionado. 22 alvará. 23 generoso. 24 sentimento. 25 immenso. 26 selva (silva). 27 uns, umas. 28 largo. 29 unico. 30 bellicoso. 31 precedente. 32 artigo. 33 agitado. 34 seguinte. 35 silencioso. 36 grave. 37 profundo. 38 amor.

30.

The Comparison of Adjectives.

The Comparative is formed by placing *mais* (more) or *menos* (less) before the Positive, as:

bello, beautiful, *mais bello*, more beautiful.

Obs. *Than* following the Comparative is rendered by *que, como,* or: *tão — como,* as — as; *não tão — como,* not so — as; before the article *que* the word *do* is often prefixed, as:

> *he mais prudente do que parece,*
> he is wiser than it appears.

The Superlative is formed

1. by placing the article before the Comparative, as:

> *o mais douto,* the most learned
> *o mais bello,* the most beautiful;

2. by adding to the Positive *issimo* (masc.) and *issima* (fem.), as: *bello,* beautiful, *bellissimo, bellissima.*

Exceptions are:

acre, tart, *acerrimo*
amigo, friendly, *amicissimo*
antigo, old, *antiquissimo*
aspero, rough, *asperrimo*
bom, good, *bonissimo*
capaz, capable, *capacissimo*
celebre, celebrated, *celeberrimo*
chão, flat, *chanissimo*
feliz, happy, *felicissimo*
fiel, faithful, *fidelissimo*
frio, cold, *frigidissimo*
humilde, humble, *humilissimo, humillimo*

máo, bad, *malissimo*
nobre, noble, *nobilissimo*
prospero, prosperous, *prosperrimo*
rico, rich, *riquissimo*
sabio, wise, *sapientissimo*
sagrado, sacred, *sacratissimo*
salubre, salutary, *saluberrimo*
simples, simple, *simplicissimo*
valente, brave, *valentissimo.*

31.

Irregular Comparisons.

Positive.		Comparative.		Superlative.	
bom,	good,	*melhor,*	better,	*optimo,*	the best,
máo,	bad,	*peior,*	worse,	*pessimo,*	the worst,
grande,	great,	*maior,*	greater,	*maximo,*	the greatest,
pequeno,	little,	*menor,*	less,	*minimo,*	the least.

Obs. The Positive and Comparative can be strengthened by placing before them:

muito, very — *assaz*, enough — *demasiado*, too, too much.

32.

Declension of the Adjective.

Masculine.

	Singular.		Plural.	
Nom.	o homem diligente		os homens diligentes	
Gen.	do homem diligente	the indus-trious man.	dos homens diligentes	the indus-trious men.
Dat.	ao homem diligente		aos homens diligentes	
Acc.	o homem diligente		os homens diligentes	
Abl.	do homem diligente		dos homens diligentes	

Feminine.

	Singular.		Plural.	
Nom.	a mulher gorda		as mulheres gordas	
Gen.	da mulher gorda	the corpu-lent woman.	das mulheres gordas	the corpu-lent women.
Dat.	á mulher gorda		ás mulheres gordas	
Acc.	a mulher gorda		as mulheres gordas	
Abl.	da mulher gorda		das mulheres gordas	

33.

Examples.

A Asia he mais grande que a Europa. A Africa he menos povoado[1] que a Europa. A rosa he mais bella que a viola[2]. A viola he menos bella que a rosa. Pedro he mais feliz do que João. O filho não he tão liberal como seu pai. A historia he tão util como agradavel. O dia he mais agradavel que a noite[3]. O seu amante he mais bello, mais moço[4] e mais rico que ella. Eu acho o agora menos lindo[5] do que quando o comprei[6]. O meu livro he tão barato[7] como o vosso. Elle he muito mais grande. Ella he pouco mais grande. Caesar he muito mais estimado[8] que Pompeo. Pompeo foi *muito menos feliz* que Caesar. Elle he o mais douto[9] dos homens. Elle he o menos douto dos homens. Ella he a mais bella das mulheres. Ella he muito amavel. Estas cadeiras [10] são feitas [11] de optima madeira [12]. Esta mulher he boa, o marido he melhor e o filho he o optimo. Elle he o felicissimo dos mortaes. O clima he saluberrimo. He homem valentissimo. O filho he rico, o pai he riquissimo. O neto [13] he máo, o primo [14] he ainda peior e o tio he o pessimo. Na margem do rio ha optimos pastos [15].

1 populated. 2 violet. 3 night. 4 young. 5 pretty. 6 to buy. 7 cheap. 8 esteemed. 9 learned. 10 chair. 11 made. 12 wood. 13 grandson. 14 cousin. 15 pasture.

34.

Exercises.

Mariana is more industrious [1] than her sister [2]. Europe is not so large as America. The wife is handsomer than her husband [3]. This horse is very beautiful, more beautiful than yours. The most fertile fields. His cousin is very rich, his uncle is still richer, and his father is the richest. The man is very bad [4], the woman is worse, and the son is the worst. This wine is good, but that one is better. She is much taller than her friend [5]. The tulip [6] is not so beautiful as the rose. The son is little, but the daughter is very little indeed *(pequenissimo)*. Our house is not so large as yours. Amelia is smaller than her brother. The best ship [7]. The worst man. The bravest knight. The simplest [8] man in the world [9]. This [10] man is very wise, and that [11] one is the wisest of all. The climate of Siberia is very cold. The summer [12] is in that country hotter and the winter [13] more rigid [14]. A great part [15] and the greater part. The turf [16] is very green [17], but the trees [18] are still greener. I do not write so well as he. This man speaks [19] as well as Cicero [20]. The English [21] horses are better than the French. Arabia has the best horses. It is commendable [22] to recommend virtue [23], but it is better to practise [24] it.

1 diligente. 2 irmãa. 3 marido. 4 máo. 5 amiga. 6 tulipa. 7 navio. 8 simples. 9 no mundo. 10 este. 11 aquelle. 12 verão. 13 inverno. 14 rigoroso. 15 parte. 16 relva. 17 verde. 18 arvore. *19 fallar.* 20 um Cicero. 21 inglez. 22 louvavel. 23 *virtude.* *24 praticar.*

35.

The Numbers (Vos Numeral).

1. The Cardinal Numbers (Numerales cardinaes).

um, fem. uma	1	vinte e nove	29
dois, dous, fem. duas	2	trinta	30
tres	3	trinta e um	31
quatro	4	quarenta	40
cinco	5	quarenta e um	41
seis	6	cincoenta	50
sete	7	sessenta	60
oito	8	setenta	70
nove	9	oitenta	80
dez	10	noventa	90
onze	11	cem, cento	100
doze	12	cento e um	101
treze	13	duzentos, fem. -as	200
quatorze	14	duzentos e um	201
quinze	15	trezentos, -as	300
dezeseis	16	quatrocentos, -as	400
dezesete	17	quinhentos	500
dezoito	18	seiscentos	600
dez e nove	19	setecentos	700
vinte	20	oitocentos	800
vinte e um	21	novecentos	900
vinte e dois	22	mil	1,000
vinte e tres	23	mil e cento	1,100
vinte e quatro	24	mil e duzentos	1,200
vinte e cinco	25	dois mil	2,000
vinte e seis	26	cem mil	100,000
vinte e sete	27	milhũa	a million
vinte e oito	28	bilhão	a billion.

Obs. Before a noun *cem* is used, before a number *cento*, as: *cem soldados*, hundred soldiers; *cento e um*, a hundred and one. The Portuguese use the Cardinal Numbers to express the date, as: *chegou a quatro de Maio,* he arrived on the fourth of May.

36.

2. The Ordinal Numbers.

primeiro	the 1 st.	*decimo oitavo*	the 18 th
segundo	the 2 nd	*decimo nono*	the 19 th
terceiro	the 3 rd	*vigesimo*	the 20 th
quarto	the 4 th	*vigesimo-primeiro*	the 21 st
quinto	the 5 th	*vigesimo-segundo*	the 22 nd
sexto	the 6 th	*trigesimo*	the 30 th
setimo	the 7 th	*quadragesimo, quaren-*	
oitavo	the 8 th	*tesimo*	the 40 th
nono	the 9 th	*qunquagesimo*	the 50 th
decimo	the 10 th	*sexagesimo*	the 60 th
undecimo, onzeno	the 11 th	*septuagesimo*	the 70 th
duodecimo	the 12 th	*octogesimo*	the 80 th
decimo terceiro	the 13 th	*nonagesimo*	the 90 th
decimo quarto	the 14 th	*centesimo*	the 100 th
decimo quinto	the 15 th	*centesimo primeiro*	the 101 st
decimo sexto	the 16 th	*millesimo*	the 1,000 th
decimo setimo	the 17 th	*ultimo*	the last.

37.

3. Fractional Numbers.

a metade, half	*um oitavo,* an eighth
o terço, the third	*uma oitava,* an eighth part
a terça parte, the third part	*tres oitavos,* three eighths
o quarto ⎫ the fourth part	*uma novena,* a ninth
a quarta parte ⎭	*uma nona parte,* a ninth part
o quinto, ⎫ the fifth part	*uma decima parte,* a tenth part
a quinta parte, ⎭	*um e meio,* one and a half
a sexta parte, the sixth part	*dous e meia,* two and a half
a setima parte, the seventh part	*tres e meia,* three and a half

38.

4. Proportional Numbers.

simples, simple
duplice \
tduplicado / double
triple \
triplice / triple
quadruplo, fourfold
quintuplo, fivefold
uma vez, once
duas vezes, twice

tres vezes, thrice
sextuplo, sixfold
septuplo, sevenfold
octuplo, eightfold
nonuplo, ninefold
decuplo, tenfold
centuplo, a hundredfold
a primeira vez, the first time.

39.

5. Collective Numbers.

um par, a pair
ambos, ambas, both
um terno, a number of 3
um quaterno, a number of 4
uma dezena, a number of 10
uma duzia, a dozen
uma quinzena, fifteen

uma sessenta, sixty
uma centena, a hundred
uma vintena, twenty
um milhar, a thousand
quintal, a hundred weight
uma quarta do arratel, a quarter of a pound.

todo, toda, tudo, all, every one; p l u r. *todos, todas.*
muito, many *tanto*, so many. — *pouco*, few.

40.

Examples.

Elle viveo [1] noventa annos [2]. Ella tem vinto e cinco annos de idade [3]. O exercito [4] he composto [5] de noventa mil e seiscentos homens. Dous mil cincocentos e trinta e quatro homens forão mortos [6] neste encontro [7]. Cem homens ficarão [8] prisioneiros [9]. Ha nesta povoação [10] mil e setecentas almas [11]. Ha mil quinhentas casas na nossa freguezia [12]. A sua carta [13] he datada [14] de vinte e dous de Abril de mil oitocentos e cincoenta e sete. Nosso tio ha de chegar [15] a treze do mez que vem. O comprimento[16] desta rua tem o dobro do da outra. Eu fiz duas vezes a volta[17] da villa a cavallo. Um terremoto[18] destruio[19] a metade da cidade. Este theatro foi queimado[20] tres vezes. Se cultivar a sua herdade[21], ella se elevará[22] em valor ao centuplo.

1 live. 2 year. 3 age. 4 army. 5 consists of. 6 killed. 7 battle. 8 remained. 9 prisoners. 10 population. 11 souls. 12 parish. 13 letter. 14 dated. 15 arrive. 16 length. 17 the round. 18 earthquake. 19 destroy. 20 burnt down. 21 inheritance. 22 to raise.

41.

Exercises.

The company[1] consists of one hundred men and the regiment[2] has six thousand men. There were collected[3] two hundred men and nearly[4] seventy women. He was the first who arrived[5]. The second was your brother. The third man I have not seen. The French army consists of 600,000 men. Within[6] eight days. He had one sister and two cousins[7] with him. This house would be worth a hundred times more. Once I have told him, but twice he has forgotten it. The first time that I had the knife ground[8]. A thousand men were killed in this battle[9]. The first day of the year[10]. To day is the first, the second, the third, the fourth of the month[11]. Twenty eggs[12]. He arrived on the fifth of July. The nineteenth century[13]. The year has 365 days. He has three sons[14] and five daughters[15].

1 companhia. 2 regimento. 3 ajuntado. 4 quasi. 5 chegar. 6 dentro. 7 prima. 8 amolar. 9 batalha. 10 anno. 11 mez. 12 ovo. 13 seculo. 14 filho. 15 filha.

42.

Pronouns.

1. Personal Pronouns.

Singular.

1st Person.	2nd Person.	3rd Person. Masc.	Fem.
N. *eu,* I	*tu,* thou	*elle,* he	*ella,* she
G. *de mim,* of me	*de ti,* of thee	*d'elle,* of him	*d'ella,* of her
D. *a mim,* to me	*a ti,}* to thee	*a elle, lhe,* to him	*a ella,* to her
Acc. *me,* me	*te, a ti,* thee	*elle,* him	*ella, a ella,* her
Abl. *de mim,}* from me / *por mim}*	*de ti }* from thee / *por ti}*	*d'elle,}* from him / *por elle,}*	*d'ella,}* from her / *por ella,}*

Plural.

N. *nós,* we	*vós,* you	*elles,* they	*ellas,* they
G. *de nos,* of us	*de vos,* of you	*d'elles,* of them	*d'ellas,* of them
D. *a nos,* to us	*a vós,* to you	*a elles, lhes,* to them	*a ellas,* to them
Acc. *nos, a nos* us	*a vos, vos,* you	*elles, a elles,* them,	*ellas,* them
Abl. *de nos.}* from us / *por nos,}*	*de vós,* from you	*d'elles,* from them	*d'ellas,* from them.

Obs. If the Pronouns *mim, ti, si, nós, vós,* are accompanied by the Preposition *com,* they are contracted thus:

com mim	into	*commigo,*	with me
com ti	-	*comtigo,*	with thee
com si	-	*comsigo,*	with him
com nós	-	*comnosco,*	with us
com vos	-	*comvosco,*	with you.

Me is generally translated by *me,* as:

speak to me, *fallai-me* — he told me, *elle disse-me*
tell me, *dizei-me* — write me, *escrevei-me.*

The reflective Pronoun *si.*

Nom. *si,*	one's self
Gen. *de si,*	of one's self
Dat. *a si,*	to one's self
Acc. *si, a si,*	one's self
Abl. *de si, por si,*	from one's self.

It is generally united to the pronoun: *mesmo* or *mesma*, as: *de si mesmo,* of one's self:

> *o homen não ama senão a si memso,* the man loves only himself.

The Portuguese also join *mesmo*, to the personal pronouns, as:

eu mesmo, I myself	*nós mesmos,* we ourselves
tu mesmo, thou thyself	*vós mesmos,* you yourselves
elle mesmo, he himself	*elles mesmos,* } they themselves
ella mesma, she herself	*ellas mesmas,* }
o homem mesmo, the man himself	*a virtude mesma,* virtue itself.

43.

2. Conjunctive Pronouns.

The following are always used in connexion with verbs:

me, me	— *nos,* us
te, thee	— *vos,* you
se, it	— *lhes,* them
lhe, him, her.	

---

isto me agrada	— it pleases me
he-me necessario	— I want it (have it necessary)
deos te ve	— God sees thee
ella se louva,	— she praises herself
eu lhe direi,	— I shall tell him *or* her
eu lhes prometti	— I have promised them.

44.

3. Mixed Pronouns

are composed of personal and conjunctive pronouns, by changing the letter *e* of the conjunctive pronoun into o and a., as:

instead of *me o* — say: *mo*

\-   - *me a* —   -   *ma*

\-   - *lhe o* —   -   *lho*

\-   - *lhe a* —   -   *lha*

\-   - *me os* —   -   *mos*

\-   - *me as* —   -   *mas*

\-   - *lhe os* —   -   *lhos*

\-   - *lhe as* —   -   *lhas*

\-   - *te o* —   -   *to*

\-   - *te a* —   -   *ta*

\-   - *te os* —   -   *tos*

\-   - *te as* —   -   *tas.*

---

dai-mo, give me (*livro,* the book)

dai-mo, give me (*cão,* the dog)

dai-ma, give me (*penna,* the pen).

entrego-to, I give it thee (*libro*)

darei-ta, I shall give it thee (*casa*)

entrego-tos, I give them to thee (*chapéos,* pl.)

darei-tas, I shall give them to thee (*peras,* pl.)

---

se o,	changes	into	*selo*	*nos os,*	changes	into	*nolos*
se a,	-	-	*sela*	*nos as,*	-	-	*nolas*
se os,	-	-	*selos*	*vos o,*	-	-	*volo*
se as,	-	-	*selas*	*vos a,*	-	-	*vola*
nos o,	-	-	*nolo*	*vos os,*	-	-	*volos*
nos a,	-	-	*nola*	*vos as,*	-	-	*volas*

Examples.

para dar-lho.	for the purpose of giving it to him
dai-mo,	give it me
eu to darei,	I shall give it to thee
entrego-to,	I hand it over to thee
dize-lho,	they told it him or her
entrega-lhos,	give them (or her) to him
elle nolo disse,	he told it us
eu volos mandarei,	I shall send them to you.

45.

4. Possessive Pronouns.

<table>
<tr><td colspan="3">Masculine.</td><td colspan="3">Feminine.</td></tr>
<tr><td colspan="2">Singular.</td><td>Plural.</td><td colspan="2">Singular.</td><td>Plural.</td></tr>
<tr><td>*meu,*</td><td>mine</td><td>*meus*</td><td>*minha,*</td><td>mine</td><td>*minhas*</td></tr>
<tr><td>*teu,*</td><td>thine</td><td>*theus*</td><td>*tua,*</td><td>thine</td><td>*tuas*</td></tr>
<tr><td>*seu,*</td><td>his</td><td>*seus*</td><td>*sua,*</td><td>hers</td><td>*suas*</td></tr>
<tr><td>*nosso,*</td><td>ours</td><td>*nossos*</td><td>*nossa,*</td><td>ours</td><td>*nossas*</td></tr>
<tr><td>*vosso,*</td><td>yours</td><td>*vossos*</td><td>*vossa,*</td><td>yours</td><td>*vossas*</td></tr>
</table>

The pronouns are declined with the definite article, as:

Masculine.

	Singular.	Plural.
	my book.	my books.
N.	*o meu livro*	*os meus livros*
G.	*do meu livro*	*dos meus livros*
D.	*ao meu livro*	*aos meus livros*
Acc.	*meu livro*	*meus livros*
Abl.	*do (pelo) meu livro*	*dos (pelos) meus livros*

Feminine.

	Singular.	Plural.
	my house.	my houses.
N.	*a minha casa*	*as minhas casas*
G.	*da minha casa*	*das minhas casas*
D.	*á minha casa*	*ás minhas casas*
Acc.	*minha casa*	*minhas casas*
Abl.	*da (pela) minha casa*	*das (pelas) minhas casas*

Examples.

The Portuguese say:

the father loves: *a seu filho,* his son
the mother loves: *a seu filho,* her son

the father loves his daughter: *o pai ama á sua filha*
the mother loves her daughter: *a mai ama á sua filha*
it is mine: *he meu*
it is thine: *he teu.*

46.

5. Demonstrative Pronouns.

Este, denotes a person or thing in our immediate neighbourhood.
Esse, denotes a person or thing a little more distant from us.
Aquelle, one still farther distant.

Singular.

	Masculine.	Feminine.	Neuter
N.	*este,* this	*esta*	*isto*
G.	*d'este,* of this	*d'esta*	*d'isto*
D.	*a este,* to this	*a esta*	*a isto*
Acc.	*este,* this	*esta*	*isto*
Abl.	*d'este,* from this	*d'esta*	*d'isto*

Plural.

	Masculine.	Feminine.	Neuter
N.	*estes,* these	*estas*	
G.	*d'estes,* of these	*d'estas*	
D.	*a estes,* to these	*a estas*	wanting
Acc.	*estes,* these	*estas*	
Abl.	*d'estes,* from these	*d'estas*	

Singular.

	Masculine.	Feminine.	Neuter
N.	*esse,* this one	*essa*	*isso*
G.	*d'esse* of this one	*d'éssa*	*d'isso*
D.	*a esse,* to this one	*a essa*	*a isso*
Acc.	*esse,* this one	*éssa*	*isso*
Ahl.	*d'esse,* from this one	*d'essa*	*d'isso*

Plural.

N.	*esses,*	these	*essas*	
G.	*d'esses,*	of these	*d'essas*	
D.	*a esses,*	to these	*a essas*	wanting
Acc.	*esses,*	these	*essas*	
Abl.	*d'esses,*	from these	*d'essas*	

Singular.

N.	*aquelle,*	that	*aquella*	*aquillo*
G.	*d'aquelle,*	of that	*d'aquella*	*d'aquillo*
D.	*áquelle,*	to that	*áquella*	*áquillo*
Acc.	*aquelle,*	that	*aquella*	*aquillo*
Abl.	*d'aquelle,*	from that	*d'aquella*	*d'aquillo*

Plural.

N.	*aquelles,*	those	*aquellas*	
G.	*d'aquelles,*	of those	*d'aquellas*	
D.	*áquelles,*	to those	*áquellas*	wanting
Acc.	*aquelles,*	those	*aquellas*	
Abl.	*d'aquelles,*	from those	*d'aquellas*	

47.

6. Relative Pronouns.

a) *Qual*, which, declined with the article *o* and *a*: *o qual, a qual*; plural: *os quaes, as quaes.*

b) *Que*, which, is used of persons and things, as:

o livro que, the book which
a arvore que, the tree which
os livros que, the books which
o mestre que ensina, the teacher who instructs
a mulher que tenho, the woman whom I have
o homem que eu amo, the man whom I love.

It is declined:

N. *que,*   who, which, what
G. *de que,*   of whom
D. *á que,*   to whom
Acc. *que,*   whom
Abl. *de que,* from whom.

e) *Quem,* is only used of persons.

Singular and Plural.

N. *quem,*   who
G. *de quem,* of whom
D. *á quem,*   to whom
Acc. *quem,*   whom
Abl. *de quem,* from whom.

d) *Cujo, cuja,* whose.

Singular.

	Masculine.		Feminine.
N.	—		—
G.	*de cujo,*	of whose	*de cuja*
D.	*a cujo,*	to whose	*a cuja*
Acc.	*cujo,*	whose	*cuja*
Abl.	*de cujo,*	whose	*de cuja*

Examples.

a pessoa cuja reputação, vós admirais.	The person whose reputation you admire.
o ceo cujo soccorro nunca falta.	The heaven whose assistance never fails.
a mulher cuja bella cara.	The woman whose beautiful face
cujas bellezas.	Whose beauties.
a cujo pai.	To whose father.

48.

7. Interrogative Pronouns.

Quem, qual, que, who, which, what?

Singular and Plural.

	Masc. and Fem.			Masc. and Fem.	
N.	*quem,*	who?	*que*		
G.	*de quem,*	of whom?	*de que*		
D.	*á quem,*	to whom?	*á que*	} what? which?
Acc.	*quem,*	whom?	*que*		
Abl.	*de quem,*	whom?	*de que*		

Singular.   Plural.

Masculine and Feminine.

	Singular			Plural	
N.	*qual,*	which?	*quaes*		
G.	*de qual,*	of which?	*de quaes*		
D.	*á qual,*	to which?	*á quaes*	} which?
Acc.	*qual,*	which?	*quaes*		
Abl.	*de qual,*	from which?	*de quaes*		

Examples.

Quem he?	Who is it?
Quem vos disse isso?	Who told that to you?
Que quereis?	What do you want?
Com que se sustenta?	What does he live upon?
Que estais fazendo?	What are you doing?
De que se faz isto?	What is this made of?
Que livro he este?	What book is this?
Que negocios tendes?	What business have you?
Que casa he?	What sort of a house is it?
De qual fallais vós?	Of whom do you speak?
Qual delles?	Which of them?
Quem or *qual dos dous?*	Which of the two?

49.

8. Indefinite Pronouns.

um, una, a, one
uns, umas, some
algum, alguma, somebody
alguns, algumas, some
nenhum, nenhuma, no one
nenhuns, nenhumas, none
cada, each
cada um, cada. uma, everyone
outro, outra, other
outros, outras, others
se, one, some one
todo, toda, all, everyone

todos, todas, all
tudo, everything
tal $\Big\}$ such
tales
qualquer | whoever
quaesquer | some one
quemquer, any one
alguem, some one
ninguem, no one
outrem, another, some one else
muitos, muitas, many.

certo, certa, a certain one
um e outro $\Big\}$ the one and the other
uma e outra

um ou outro
uns ou outros $\Bigg\}$ the one or the other
uma ou outra
umas ou outras

nenhum nem outro
nenhuns nem outros $\Bigg\}$ neither the one nor the other.
nenhuma nem outra
nenhumas nem outras

50.

Examples.

Eu sou pobre [1] e tu es rico. Eu amo [2] e tu amas tambem, elle ama, elles amão. Ella nunca [3] traz [4] dinheiro comsigo. Isto me agrada [5]. Ella se louva [6]. Eu lhe direi [7]. Cortailhe [8] as azas [9]. Comprei o cavallo e montei-o [10]. Louvavel [11] he aconselhar [12] a virtude, mas melhor he pratica-la [13]. Assenta *no que lhe digo.* A sua perda [14]. Este vento [15] he favoravel [16].

Louva-se lhe a generosidade [17]. Esta flor [18] não he do meu jardím, he do teu. O que lhe digo he verdade. O ceo cujo soccorro nunca falta. Carlos foi grande, Frederico ambicioso, este valente [19], aquelle poderoso [20]. Aquelles que desprezão [21] a sciencia [22] não conhecem [23] o valor d'ella. A providencia não abençoa [24] o trabalho [25] d'aquelles que desprezão os seus melhores amigos. Aquelles taes que não amão a virtude, não a conhecem. O homem que eu amo. O meu livro está na mesa. De todas as obras de engenho, nenhuma ha que não tenha o seu defeito [26]. A pessoa cuja reputação [27] vós admirais [28]. Um tal velhaco [29] deve [30] ser castigado [31]. Aprendem-se [32] com mais facilidade [33] as cousas que se comprehendem, do que as que se não comprehendem.

1 poor. 2 love. 3 never. 4 *trazer*, to carry. 5 *agradar*, to please. 6 praise. 7 *dizer*, to say. 8 to cut, to trim. 9 the wing. 10 to mount. 11 praiseworthy. 12 to advise. 13 to practice. 14 the loss. 15 the wind. 16 favorable. 17 generosity. 18 flower. 19 valiant. 20 powerful. 21 to despise. 22 sciences. 23 to know. 24 to bless. 25 labour. 26 imperfection, fault. 27 reputation. 28 to admire. 29 scoundrel. 30 ought. 31 to punish. 32 *aprender*, to learn. 33 facility.

51.

Esta batalha[1] decidirá[2] a sorte[3] da campanha[4]. Este homem he sabio [5], aquelle he valente. Esta arvore he nova [6], essa velha, aquella foi desarraigada [7]. Este cavallo he arabe, est'outro he andaluz, aquell'outro he inglez. O culto [8] dos idolos [9], o qual he tão antigo como absurdo. As molestias[10] contra as quaes a medicina he impotente. Qual he o caracter distinctivo dos templos gothicos? O estado cujo governo, cujos habitantes, cuja religião, cujas instituições nos parecem[11] preferiveis [12]. O marido, cuja mulher, cujas filhas são virtuosas, deve reputar-se feliz. O amigo de cuja casa venho. Quem descobrio a America? Quem fórão os primeiros habitantes da Grecia? Que homem he esse que vejo na estrada. Nenhum homem he izento[13] de paixões [14]. Elle em generosidade não cede a ninguem. Um morreo na India, o outro em França. Não faze a outrem o que não quizeras te fizessem a ti. Em taes circumstancias. A conclusão foi tal qual eu a esperava. Elle fallou [15] contra mim. Quaes são os requisitos de um bom pintor?

1 battle. 2 to decide. 3 the issue. 4 the campaign. 5. wise. 6 young, new. 7 uprooted. 8 worshipping. 9 idols. 10 disease 11 appear. 12 excellent. 13 exempt. 14 passion. 15 *fallar* to speak.

52.

Exercises.

I have a dress [1]. He has stockings [2]. She has shoes [3]. We have money [4]. You have houses. They have chairs [5]. He received the money from thee. This horse is handsomer than that one. This is white [6] and that is blue [7]. The wife of my uncle. The house of my sister. The woman whose husband was killed [8]. The man whose wife is so like [9] your sister. What are the requisites [10] to make a great minister [11]? Who has told you this? Of whom did you learn this news? What animals are there on this island [12]? The man who wishes to be esteemed [13] must esteem himself. All men must [14] die [15]. Every man and every woman received a present [16].

1 vestido. 2 meia. 3 sapato. 4 dinheiro. 5 cadeira. 6 branco 7 azul. 8 morto, matado. 9 igualar. 10 requisito. 11 ministro. 12 ilha. 13 estimar, respeitar. 14 dever. 15 morrer. 16 dom, dativa.

53.

Exercises.

I see nobody. Nobody answers me. The one lives in Holland [1] and the other in Germany [2]. The one is an honest man [3] and the other is a scoundrel [4]. Neither [5] the one nor [5] the other. This man is a Spaniard [6], the other an Englishman [7], and that one a German [8]. Each one of these Indians. This is good [9] and that is bad [10]. This man only loves himself [11]. *Many authors maintain* [12]. In certain seasons [13] and in certain

times [14]. A certain man said. A certain person. Such a man.
The panic [15] was such that everyone fled [16]. Any one of the
conspirators [17].

1 Hollanda. 2 Allemanha. 3 homem de bem. 4 velhaco. 5 *neither
— nor*, nem — nem. 6 Hespanhol. 7 Inglez. 8 Allemão. 9
bom. 10 máo. 11 amar a si-mesmo, *to love one's self.* 12 af-
firmar. 13 estação. 14 tempo. 15 terror. 16 fugir. 17 con-
jurado.

PART II.

Collection of Words.

1. The Universe.

Deos, God
o creador, the creator
o mundo, the world
o firmamento, the sky
um astro, a star
o sol, the sun
um raio de sol, a sunbeam
a lua, the moon
o luar, the moonlight
uma nuvem, a cloud
uma estrella, a star
o céo, os céos, the heaven
a nascer do sol, sunrise
o pór do sol, sunset
um cometa, a comet

o arco iris, the rainbow
o trovão, the thunder
o calor, the heat
um relampago, a flash of light-
o fogo, the fire　　　　ning
o frio, the cold
a geada, the frost
o gelo, the ice
a luz, the light
a neve, the snow
o obscuridade, the darkness
uma trovoada, a storm
a chuva, the rain
o tempo, the weather
o vento, the wind.

2. The Seasons.

Primavera, spring
estio, verão, summer
outono, autumn
inverno, winter
Janeiro, January

Fevereiro, February
Março, March
Abril, April,
Maio, May
Junho, June.

Julho, July
Agosto, August
Septembro, September
Outubro, October
Novembro, November
Dezembro, December
Segunda feira, Monday
Terça feira, Tuesday
Quarta feira, Wednesday
Quinta feira, Thursday
Sexta feira, Friday
Sabbado, Saturday
Domingo, Sunday
um seculo, a century
um anno, a year
o anno passado, the last year
o anno que vem, the next year
um moz, a month
uma semana, a week
um dia, a day
uma hora, an hour
meia hora, half an hour

hora e meia, an hour and a half
um quarto d'hora, a quarter of an hour
um minuto, a minute
um segundo, a second
o despontar do dia, the day-break
a madrugada, the morning
a manhã, the forenoon
meio-dia, noon
a tarde, the afternoon
o pór do sol, sunset
a entrada, the evening
a noite, the night
meia noite, midnight
hoje, to-day
hontem, yesterday
antes d'hontem, the day before yesterday
á manhã, to-morrow
o fim, the end, close.

---

3. Water.

Uma bahia, a bay
agua corrente, running water
agua enxarcada, stagnant water
agua morta, standing water
agua doce, sweet water
agua do mar, sea water
um lago, a pond
um rio, a river
um lago, uma lagoa, a lake
um charco, a pool
a maré, the tide
maré alta, high water
maré baixa, low water
o mar, the sea
mar perigoso, a rough sea
as ondas, the waves

um regato, a brook
um nascente, a spring
uma torrente, a torrent
as ondas, the billows
um barco de vapor, a steamer
um brigue, a brig
uma fragata, a frigate
um navio mercante, a merchant ship
um navio de guerra, a man of war
uma ancora, an anchor
a rabadilha, the stern
a proa, the head
um remo, an oar
a cana do leme, the helm

um masto, a mast	*umá vela*, a sail
a bandeira, the flag	*o velame*, the sails.
a tolda, the deck	

---

4. Individuals and Relations.

Um homem, a man	*uma irmã*, a sister
uma mulher, a woman	*um tio*, an uncle
as mulheres, women	*umą tia*, an aunt
uma mulher casada, a wife	*um sobrinho*, a nephew
um menino, a child	*uma sobrinha*, a niece
um moço, a boy	*um primo*, a cousin
uma rapariga, a girl	*uma familia*, a family
um mancebo, a young man	*os parentes*, the parents
uma moça, a young maid	*o marido*, the husband
um velho, an old man	*a esposa*, the wife
uma velha, an old woman	*o noivo*, the bridegroom
o avô, the grandfather	*a noiva*, the bride
a avô, the grandmother	*o sogro*, the father-in-law
o pai, the father	*a sogra*, the mother-in-law
a mai, the mother	*o genro*, the son-in-law
o filho, the son	*a nóra*, the daughter-in-law
a filha, the daughter	*um cunhado*, a brother-in-law
um irmão, a brother	*uma cunhada*, a sister-in-law.

---

5. The Human Body.

A pelle, the skin	*um joelho*, a knee
a barba, the beard	*uma perna*, a leg
a boca, the mouth	*uma face*, a cheek
um braço, an arm	*a lingua*, the tongue
um cabello, a hair	*um beiço*, a lip
o coração, the heart	*uma mão*, a hand
o pescoço, the neck	*o nariz*, the nose
um dente, a tooth	*um olho*, an eye
um dedo, a finger	*uma orelha*, an ear
a espalda, the back	*um pé*, a foot
uma ecpadoa, a shoulder	*o pulso*, the fist
o estomago, the stomach	*a cabeça*, the head.
a face, the face	

---

6. House and Furniture.

Uma casa, a house
um palacio, a palace
uma quinta, a country house
uma livraria, a library
um quarto, a room
um quarto de dormir, a bed-room
a escada, the staircase
uma janella, a window
o tecto de estuque, the ceiling
o solho, the floor
uma porta, a door
uma fechadura, a lock
a chave, the key
uma sala baixa, a parlour
uma sala da jantar, a dining room
uma sala, a drawing-room
uma campaïnha, the bell
uma mobilia, furniture
uma cadeira, a chair

um castiçal, a candlestick
uma vella de sebo, a candle
uma cheminé, a chimney
uma comoda, a chest of drawers
um espelho de sala, a looking glass
um candieiro, a lamp
uma cama, a bed
uma cortina, a curtain
uma papeleira, a writing-desk
um sofa, a sofa
uma mesa, a table
um quadro, a picture
um tapete, a carpet
as gavetas, a chest of drawers
uma toalha de mesa, a table cloth
uma colher, a spoon
uma colherinha, a tea spoon
um garfo, a fork
uma faca, a knife.

7. Trees, Shrubs etc.

Os cereaes, corn
a aveia, oats
o feno, hay
o trigo candeal, wheat
a herva, grass
a batata, potatoe
o arroz, rice
uma bétula, a birch-tree
uma ceregeira, a cherry-tree
uma azinheira, an oak

uma figueira, a fig-tree
uma faia, a beech-tree
uma hera, ivy
um olmo, an elm
um chopo, a poplar
um pinheiro, a pine
um abeto, a fir
um salgueiro, a willow
um til, a lime-tree.

8. Fruits and Flowers.

Um damasco, an apricot
uma cereja, a cherry
uma castanha, a chestnut

um limão, a lemon
um figo, a fig
um morango, a strawberry

uma groselha, a currant
groselha de bagos grossos, a gooseberry
uma noz, a nut
uma pera, a pear
uma maçã, an apple
o lirio, the lily
a margarita, the daisy

o lirio dos valles, the lily of the valley
o cravo, the pink
a papoula, the poppy
a primavera, the primrose
a rosa, the rose
a tulipa, the tulip
a violeta, the violet.

---

9. Dress.

Uma camiza, a shirt
umas ceroulas, drawers
uma camizola, an underwaistcoat
uns calções, breeches
um colete, a waistcoat
uma casaca, a coat
um capote, a cloak
um chapéo, a hat
uma bota, a boot
uma anagoa, a petticoat
um vestido, a gown
uma touca, a bonnet
um veo, a veil
um collar, a necklace

um brinco, an ear-ring
pulseiras, bracelets
uma meia, a stocking
um sapato, a shoe
uma luva, a glove
uma bolsa, a purse
um annel, a ring
pós, powder
sabão, soap
um toalha de mãos, a towel
um pente, a comb
uma escova, a brush
uma escova de dentes, a toothbrush.

---

10. Town and Country.

Uma cidade, a town
uma aldea, a village
os arrabaldes, the surburbs
um candieiro de gaz, a gas lamp
a calçada, the pavement
uma praça, a square
uma ponte, a bridge
um passeio, a walk
um farol, a lamp

uma rua, a street
um bosquesinho, a thicket
um campo, a field
uma cavalhariça, a stable
uma floresta } a forest
uma selva }
uma sebe, a hedge
um jardim, a garden
um almargeal, a meadow
um vergel, an orchard.

---

11. Animals.

Um cervo, a stag	*um burro*, a donkey
um crocodillo, a crocodile	*uma ovelha*, a sheep
um elephante, an elephant	*um borrego*, a lamb
um coelho, a rabbit	*um gato*, a cat
uma lebre, a hare	*um cão*, a dog
um lião, a lion	*um cavallo*, a horse
um leopardo, a leopard	*um macho*, a mule
um lobo, a wolf	*uma vaca*, a cow
um urso, a bear	*um bezerro*, a calf
uma panthera, a panther	*um boi*, an ox
um rato, a rat	*um leitão*, a pig
uma raposa, a fox	*o gado*, cattle
um mono, a monkey	*gado vacum*, herds
um tigre, a tiger	*godo meudo*, flocks.

12. Birds, Fishes and Insects.

Um pata, a duck	*uma perca*, a perch
um gallo, a cock	*um salmão*, a salmon
uma gallinha, a hen	*um linguado*, a sole
um ganso, a goose	*uma truta*, a trout
um pombo, a pigeon	*um rodavalho*, a turbot
uma aguia, an eagle	*uma abelha*, a bee
uma calhandra, a lark	*uma aranhá*, a spider
uma cegonha, a stork	*um sapo*, a toad
um corvo, a raven	*uma borboleta*, a butterfly
um cisne, a swan	*uma serpente*, a serpent
uma andorinha, a swallow	*um escaravelho*, a beetle
um roussinol, a nightingale	*uma formiga*, an ant
uma enguia, an eel	*uma rã*, a frog
uma carpa, a carp	*uma vespa*, a wasp
um harenque, a herring	*uma mosca*, a fly
uma lagosta, a lobster	*um bicho*, a worm
uma ostra, an oyster	*uma vibora*, a viper
uma sarda, a mackerel	*uma cobra*, an adder.

Easy Dialogues.*)

1. Eating and Drinking.

Are you hungry?	*Vm. tem fome?*
I have a good appetite.	*Tenho boa vontade de comer.*
I am very hungry.	*Tenho bastante fome.*
Eat something.	*Coma alguma cousa.*
What will you eat?	*Que ha de Vm. comer?*
What do you wish to eat?	*Que é o que tem vontade de comer?*
You do not eat.	*O senhor naõ come.*
I beg your pardon, I eat very heartily.	*Com perdaõ de Vm., eu como muito bem.*
I have eaten very heartily.	*Tenho comido bastante.*
I have dined with a good appetite.	*Jantei de boa vontade.*
Have another piece.	*Coma ainda mais alguma cousa.*
I can eat no more.	*Naõ comerei mais nada.*
Are you thirsty?	*Tem Vm. séde?*
Are you not thirsty?	*Naõ tem Vm. séde?*
I am very thirsty.	*Tenho bastante sêde.*
I am dying of thirst.	*Estou morrendo de séde.*
Let us drink.	*Toça a beber.*
Give me something to drink.	*De-me de beber.*
Will you drink a glass of wine?	*Quer Vm. beber um copo de vinho?*
Drink a glass of beer.	*Tome um capo de cerveja.*
Drink another glass of wine.	*Beba mais esse copo de vinho.*
Sir, I drink to your health.	*Bebo a sua saude.*
I have the honour to drink your health.	*Tenho a honra de beber á sua saúde.*

---

*) The student who is desirous of acquiring fluency in Portuguese Conversation ought to use: Portuguese and English Idiomatic Phrases and Dialogues by Monteiro. London, published by Franz Thimm. It contains the most necessary Phrases and Idiomatic Dialogues, which are in daily use in Portugal and Brasil.

2. Going and Coming.

Where are you going?	*Onde vai Vm.?*
I am going home.	*Vou para casa.*
I was going to your house.	*Hia á sua casa.*
From whence do you come?	*Donde vem Vm.?*
I come from my brother's.	*Venho de casa de meu irmão.*
I am coming from church.	*Venho da igreja.*
I have just left the school.	*Saio da escola.*
Will you come with me?	*Quer Vm. vir commigo?*
Whither do you wish to go?	*Onde quer Vm. hir?*
We will take a walk.	*Hiremos passeiar.* / *Hiremos fazer um passeio.*
With all my heart; most willingly.	*Quero, pois naõ. Com muito gosto.*
Which way shall we go?	*Per onde iremos?*
Any way you like.	*Para aquella que quizer.*
Let us go into the park.	*Vamos a tapada.*
Let us take your brother in our way.	*Vamos ter de caminho com seu irmão.*
As you please.	*Como queira.*
Is Mr. B. at home?	*O senhor B. está em casa?*
He is gone out.	*Está fóra.*
He is not at home.	*Naõ esta em casa.*
Can you tell us where he is gone?	*Pode Vm. dizer-me para onde foi?*
I cannot tell you precisely.	*Naõ saberei dizer-lhe ao certo.*
I think he is gone to see his sister.	*Creio que foi ver a irmã.*
Do you know when he will come back?	*Sabe Vm. quando ha de voltar?*
No, he said nothing about it when he went out.	*Naõ: partio sem m'odizer.*
Then we must go without him.	*Entaõ ir-nos hemos sem elle.*

---

3. Questions and Answers.

Come nearer; I have something to tell you.	*Venha ca, tenho que lhe dizer uma cousa.*
I have a word to say to you.	*Tenho que lhe dizer duas palavras.*

Listen to me.	*Escute-me.*
I want to speak to you.	*Tenho desejo de lhe fallar.*
What is it you want?	*Que ha de novo para o seu serviço?*
I am speaking to you.	*É com Vm. que fallo.*
I am not speaking to you.	*Naõ é com Vm. que eu fallo.*
What do you say?	*Que diz Vm.?*
What did you say?	*Que disse Vm.?*
I say nothing.	*Naõ disse nada.*
Do you hear?	*Entende?*
Do you hear what I say?	*Entende Vm. o que digo?*
Do you understand me?	*Entende-me Vm.?*
Will you be so kind as to repeat .. ?	*Quer Vm. repetil'o?*
I understand you well.	*Eu bem o entendo.*
Why do you not answer me?	*Por que me naõ responde?*
Do you not speak Portuguese?	*Vm. naõ falla portuguez?*
Very little, Sir.	*Muito pouco, senhor.*
I understand it a little, but I do not speak it.	*Entendo-o um pouco, porém naõ fallo.*
Speak louder.	*Falle mais alto.*
Do not speak so loud.	*Naõ falle taõ alto.*
Do not make so much noise.	*Naõ faça tanta bulha.*
Hold your tongue.	*Calle-se.*
Did you not tell me that .. ?	*Naõ me disse Vm. que?*
Who told you that?	*Quem lhe disse isto?*
They told me so.	*Disseraõ-me.*
Somebody has told it me.	*Disse-m'o certa pessoa.*
I have heard it.	*Ouvi dizer.*
What do you wish to say?	*Que quer Vm. dizer?*
For what is that good?	*Para que é bom isto?*
What do you call that?	*Como chama Vm. a isto?*
Do you know Mr. G.?	*Conhece Vm. o senhor G.?*
I know him by sight.	*Conheço-o de vista.*
I know him by name.	*Conheço-o de nome.*

---

4. The Age.

How old are you?	*Que idade tem Vm.?*
How old is your brother?	*Que idade tem o senhor seu irmão.*

I am twelve years old	*Tenho doze annos.*
I am ten years and six months old	*Tenho dés annos e meió.*
Next month I shall be sixteen years old	*Hei de fazer desaseis annos no mez que vem.*
I was thirteen years old last week.	*Fiz treze annos a semana passada.*
You do not look so old.	*Vm. naõ me parecia ter tanta idade.*
You look older.	*Vm. parecia ter mais idade.*
I thought you were older.	*Cuidava que era mais velho.*
I did not think you were so old.	*Naõ cuidava que tivese tanta idade.*
How old may your uncle be?	*Que idade tem seu tio?*
He may be sixty years old.	*Poderá ter sessenta annos.*
He is about sixty years old.	*Tem obra de sessenta annos.*
He is more than fifty years old.	*Tem mais de cincoenta annos.*
He is a man of fifty and upwards.	*É um homem de cincoenta e tantos annos.*
He may be sixty or there abouts.	*Poderá ter cousa de sessanta annos.*
He is above eighty.	*Tem mais de oitenta annos.*
That is a great age.	*É uma idade assás adiantada.*
Is he so old?	*É taõ idoso como isto?*
He begins to grow old.	*Commença a fazer-se velo.*

---

5. The Time.

What o'clock is it?	*Que horas saõ?*
Pray tell me what time it is?	*Tenha a bondade de dizer-me que horas saõ.*
It is one o'clock.	*É uma hora.*
It is past one.	*É uma hora passada.*
It has struck one.	*É uma hora ja dada*
It is a quarter past one.	*É uma hora e um quarto.*
It is half past one.	*É hora e meia.*
It wants ten minutes to two.	*Saõ duas horas menos dés minutos.*
It is not yet two o'clock.	*Ainda naõ deraõ duas horas.*

<table>
<tr><td>It is only twelve o'clock.</td><td>Naõ é mais que meiodia.</td></tr>
<tr><td>It is almost three o'clock.</td><td>Saõ perto te tres horas.</td></tr>
<tr><td>It is on the stroke of three.</td><td>Saõ tres horas em ponto.</td></tr>
<tr><td>It is going to strike three.</td><td>Está a dar tres horas.</td></tr>
<tr><td>It is ten minutes past three.</td><td>Saõ tres horas e dés minutos.</td></tr>
<tr><td>The clock is going to strike.</td><td>O relogio está para dar horas.</td></tr>
<tr><td>There is the clock striking.</td><td>O relogio está dando horas.</td></tr>
<tr><td>It is not late.</td><td>Naõ é tarde.</td></tr>
<tr><td>It is later than I thought.</td><td>É mais tarde do que eu cuidava.</td></tr>
<tr><td>I did not think it was so late.</td><td>Naõ cuidava que fosse taõ tarde.</td></tr>
</table>

---

6. The Weather.

<table>
<tr><td>What kind of weather is it?</td><td>Que especie de tempo faz?</td></tr>
<tr><td>It is bad weather.</td><td>Faz máo tempo.</td></tr>
<tr><td>It is cloudy.</td><td>Faz um tempo escuro.</td></tr>
<tr><td>It is dreadful weather.</td><td>Faz um tempo horrivel.</td></tr>
<tr><td>It is fine weather.</td><td>Faz bom tempo.</td></tr>
<tr><td>We are going to have a fine day.</td><td>Havemos de ter um optimo dia.</td></tr>
<tr><td>It is dewy.</td><td>Ha muito orvalho.</td></tr>
<tr><td>It is foggy.</td><td>Faz neova.</td></tr>
<tr><td>It is rainy weather.</td><td>Faz um tempo chuvoso.</td></tr>
<tr><td>It threatens to rain.</td><td>O tempo está embrulhado.</td></tr>
<tr><td>The sky becomes very cloudy.</td><td>O céo se esconde.</td></tr>
<tr><td>The sky is getting very dark.</td><td>O céo se escurece.</td></tr>
<tr><td>The sun is coming out.</td><td>O sol começa a apparecer.</td></tr>
<tr><td>The weather is clearing up again.</td><td>O tempo principia a concertar-se.</td></tr>
<tr><td>It is very warm.</td><td>Faz bastante calma.</td></tr>
<tr><td>It is sultry.</td><td>Faz uma calma que abafa.</td></tr>
<tr><td>It is very mild.</td><td>Faz um tempo bem brando.</td></tr>
<tr><td>It is cold.</td><td>Faz frio.</td></tr>
<tr><td>It is excessively cold.</td><td>Faz um frio terrivel.</td></tr>
<tr><td>It is raw weather.</td><td>Faz um tempo frio e juntamente humido.</td></tr>
<tr><td>It rains.</td><td>Chove</td></tr>
</table>

It has been raining.	*Choveo.*
It is going to rain.	*Está para chover.*
I feel some drops of rain.	*Sinto alguns choviscos.*
There are some drops of rain falling.	*Caem algumas gotas d'agua.*
It hails.	*Cae pedra.*
It snows; it is snowing.	*Neva. Está chovendo neve.*
It has been snowing.	*Cahio bastante neve.*
It snows in large flakes.	*Cahe neve em frocos.*
It freezes.	*Géla.*
It has frozen.	*Cahio geada.*
It begins to thaw.	*O tempo começa a abrandar-se.*
It thaws.	*Ha degelo.*
It is very windy.	*Faz bastante vento.*
The wind is very high.	*Faz uma grande ventania.*
There is no air stirring.	*Naõ ha viraçaõ.*
It lightens.	*Está fazendo relampagos.*
It has lightened all night.	*Toda esta noite fez relampagos.*
It thunders.	*Troveja.*
The thunder roars.	*Esta trovejando.*
The thunderbolt has fallen.	*Cahio um raio.*
It is stormy weather.	*O tempo ameaça trovoada.*
We shall have a thunder-storm.	*Havemus de ter alguma trovoada.*
The sky begins to clear up.	*O céo começa a limpar-se.*
The weather is very unsettled.	*O tempo está bem inconstante.*
It is very muddy.	*Faz bastante lama.*
It is very dusty.	*Ha muita poeira,*
It is very slippery.	*Escorrega muito.*
It is bad walking.	*Faz máo tempo para se sahir.*
It is day-light.	*Faz dia.*
It is dark.	*Faz escuro.*
It is night.	*Faz noite.*
It is moon-light.	*Faz luar.*
Do you think it will be fine weather?	*Cuida Vm. que teremos bom tempo?*
I do not think that it will rain.	*Creio que não ha de chover.*
I am afraid it will rain.	*Tenho medo que chova.*
I fear so.	*Eu assim o creio.*

---

7. Salutation.

Good morning, Sir.	*Bons dias, senhor.*
I wish you good morning.	*Tenha Vm. bons dias.*
How do you do? How are you?	*Como está Vm.?*
Do you continue in good health?	*Está sempre de saúde?*
Pretty good; and how are you?	*Muito bem, e Vm.?*
Are you well?	*Vm. está bem disposto?*
Very well, and you?	*Muito bem, e Vm.?*
I am perfectly well.	*Acho-me as mil maravilhas.*
And how is it with you?	*E Vm. cómo vai de saúde?*
As usual.	*Como de costume.*
Pretty well, thank God.	*Assas bem, graças a Deus.*
I am very happy to see you well.	*Estou encantado de o ver em perfeita saúde.*

---

8. The Visit.

There is a knock.	*Batem a porta.*
Somebody knocks.	*Alguem está batendo a porta.*
Go and see who it is.	*Vai ver quem é.*
Go and open the door.	*Vai abrir a porta.*
It is Mrs. B.	*É a senhora B.*
I wish you good morning.	*Tenha Vm. muito bons dias.*
I am happy to see you.	*Estou encantado de a ver.*
I have not seen you this age.	*Ha um seculo que naõ a hei visto.*
It is a novelty to see you.	*É milagre veľa.*
Pray, sit down.	*Queira assentar-se.*
Sit down if you please.	*Tenha a bondade de assentar-se.*
Take a seat.	*Queira ter o incommodo de assentar-se.*
Give a chair to the lady.	*Dé uma cadeira á senhora.*

Will you stay and take some dinner with us?	*Quer Vm. ficar para jantar comnosco.*
I cannot stay.	*Naõ posso domorar-me.*
I only came in to see how you are.	*Entrei sómente para saber da sua saúde.*
I must go.	*Naõ me posso domorar mais.*
You are in a great hurry.	*Vm. tem muita pressa.*
Why are you in such a hurry?	*Que pressa é esta?*
I have a great many things to do.	*Tenho muito que fazer.*
Surely you can stay a little longer.	*Vm. bem pode demorar-se mais una instante.*
I will stay longer another time.	*Em outra vez ficarei mais tempo.*
I thank you for your visit.	*Receba os meus agradecimentos pela visita.*
I hope to see you soon again.	*Espero de o ver bem cédo.*

---

9. Breakfast.

Have you breakfasted?	*Vm. já almoçou?*
Not yet.	*Ainda naõ.*
You have come just in time.	*Chega em boa occasiaõ.*
You will breakfast with us.	*Almoçará comnosco.*
Breakfast is ready.	*O almoço está prompto.*
Do you drink tea or coffee?	*Toma Vm. chá, ou café?*
Would you prefer chocolate?	*Gosta talvez mais de chocolate?*
I prefer coffee.	*Prefiro o café.*
What can I offer you?	*Que lhe poderei offerecer?*
Here are rolls and toast.	*Ahi tem paõ e fatias.*
What do you like best?	*De qual gosta mais?*
I shall take a roll.	*Comerei um destes pãezinhos.*
How do you like the coffee?	*Como acha Vm. o café?*
Is the coffee strong enough?	*Acha Vm. o café com bastante força?*
It is excellent.	*Acho-o excellente.*
Is there enough sugar in it?	*Tem assucar sufficiente?*

| If there is not, do not make any ceremony. | *Se não tem o que é mister, não faça ceremonias.* |
| Act as if you were at home. | *Faça como se estivesse em sua casa.* |

---

10. Before Dinner.

At what time do we dine to-day?	*A que horas jantamos hoje?*
We shall dine at four o'clock.	*Devemos jantar ás quatro.*
We shall not dine before five o'clock.	*Nem antes das cinco o faremos.*
Shall we have anybody to dinner to-day?	*Teremos hoje alguem de fóra?*
Do you expect company?	*Espera Vm. gente?*
I expect Mr. B.	*Espero pelo senhor B.*
Mr. D. has promised to come if the weather permits.	*O senhor por D. prometteo de vir, se o tempo permitisse.*
Have you given orders for dinner?	*Deo Vm. já os ordens para o jantar?*
What have you ordered for dinner?	*Que encommendou Vm. para o jantar?*
Have you sent for fish?	*Mandou Vm. vir peixe?*
I could not get any fish.	*Naõ pude haver peixe.*
I fear we shall have a very indifferent dinner.	*Quer me parecer, que havemos de ter um máo jantar.*
We must do as we can.	*Faremos como podermos.*

---

11. The Dinner.

To what shall I help you?	*Que quer que lhe sirva?*
Will you take a little soup?	*Quer uma pouca de sopa?*
I thank you. I will trouble you for a little beef.	*Obrigado, aceitarei um pouco de vaca.*
It looks so very nice.	*Tem mui boa apparencia.*

Which part do you like best? — *De que parte gosta mais?*

I hope you like this piece. — *Espero que este bocado é a seu gosto.*

Gentlemen, you have dishes near you. — *Senhores, Vm. tem dous pratos diante de si.*

Help yourselves. — *Sirvão-se.*

Take without ceremony what you like best. — *Sirvaõ-se sem ceremonia daquillo de que mais gostarem.*

Would you like a little of this roast meat? — *Quer um pouco deste assado?*

Will you have some fat? — *Gosta de gordura?*

Give me some of this lean, if you please. — *Dé-me do que naõ tem gordura, por quem é.*

How do you like the roast-meat? — *Que tal acha o ássado?*

It is excellent, delicious. — *Excellente.*

What will you take with your meat? — *Que quer Vm. comer com a carne?*

Shall I help you to some vegetables? — *Posso servir-lhe alguma hortaliça?*

Will you take peas or cauliflower? — *Quer Vm. ervilhas ou couves flores?*

It is quite indifferent to me. — *Gosto tanto d'um, como d'outro,*

I shall send you a piece of this fowl. — *Vou servir-lhe desta ave.*

No, thank you, I can eat no more. — *Muito obrigado, tenho comido sufficiente.*

You are a poor eater. — *Vm. come mui pouco.*

You eat nothing. — *Vm. naõ come nada.*

I beg your pardon, I do honour to your dinner. — *Pelo contrario como sufficiente.*

You may take away. — *Podem tirar a mesa.*

---

12. Tea.

Have you carried in the tea-things?	*Trouxeste tudo quanto é mister para o chá?*
Everything is on the table.	*Está tudo na mesa.*
Does the water boil?	*A agua está a ferver?*
Tea is ready.	*O chá está prompto.*
They are waiting for you.	*Estamos á sua espera.*
Here I am.	*Eis-me prompto.*
We have not cups enough.	*As chicaras naõ saõ sufficientes.*
We want two more cups and saucers.	*É mister mais duas.*
Bring another tea-spoon and a saucer.	*Falta tambem uma colher e um pires.*
You have not brought in the sugar-tongs.	*Esqueces-te de trazer a tenaz do assucar.*
Do you take cream?	*Toma Vm. leite?*
The tea is so strong.	*O chá está muito forte.*
I shall thank you for a little more milk.	*Pedir-lhe hei mais um pouco de leite.*
Here are cakes and muffins.	*Ahi tem bolos, e bolachas.*
Do you prefer some bread and butter?	*Tal vez queira antes fatias de paõ com manteiga?*
I shall take a slice of bread and butter.	*Aceitarei uma fatia de paõ com manteiga.*
Pass the plate this way.	*Passe para cá o prato.*
Ring the bell, if you please.	*Toque a campainha.*
Will you kindly ring the bell?	*Tenha a bondade de tocar a campainha?*
We want some more water.	*É nos mister mais agua.*
Bring it as quickly as possible.	*Traze-as o mais de pressa possivel.*
Take the plate with you.	*Leva ao mesmo tempo este prato.*
Is your tea sweet enough?	*O seu chá tem o assucar sufficiente?*
Have I put sugar enough in your tea?	*Naõ sei se deitei bastante assucar no seu chá?*
It is excellent.	*Está muy bem temperado.*
I do not like it quite so sweet.	*Naõ gosto delle muito doce.*

Your tea is very good.	*O seu chá é muito bom.*
Where do you buy it?	*Onde o compra?*
I buy it at . . .	*Compro-o em casa de . . .*
Have you already done?	*Vm. naõ quer mais chá?*
You will take another cup.	*Vm. ha de tomar mais uma chicara.*
I shall pour you out half a cup.	*Vou dar-lhe uma meia chicara.*
You will not refuse me.	*Espero qui naõ a ha de engeitar.*
I have already drunk three cups, and I never drink more.	*Já tomei tres chicaras e nunca tomo mais.*

SECOND COURSE.

Verbs.

The Auxiliary Verbs.

1.

Ter and **Haver, to have.**

Infinitive Mood.

Present.	*ter*	or *haver,*	to have.
Past.	*ter tido*	- *ter havido,*	to have had.
Gerund.	*tendo*	- *havendo,*	having.
Participles.	*tido, tida*	- *havido, havida,*	had.

Indicative Mood.

Present.

eu tenho	or *hei,*	I have
tu tens	- *has,*	thou hast
elle or *ella tem*	- *ha,*	he or she has
nós temos	- *havemos* or *hemos,*	we have
vós tendes	- *haveis,*	you have
elles or *ellas tem*	- *hão,*	they have.

Imperfect.

tinha	or *havia,*	I had
tinhas	- *havias,*	thou hadst
tinha	- *havia,*	he had
tinhamos	- *haviamos,*	we had
tinheis	- *havieis,*	you had
tinhão	- *havião,*	they had.

Past definite.

tive	or *houve,*	I have had
tiveste	- *houveste,*	thou hast had
teve	- *houve,*	he has had
tivemos	- *houvemos,*	we have had
tivestes	- *houvestes,*	you have had
tiverão	- *houverão,*	they have had.

Past indefinite.

tenho tido	or *tenho havido,*	
tens tido	- *tens havido,*	
tem tido	- *tem havido,*	I have had.
temos tido	- *temos havido,*	
tendes tido	- *tendes havido,*	
tem tido	- *tem havido,*	

Past anterior.

tivera	or *houvera,*	I had had
tiveras	- *houveras,*	thou hadst had
tivera	- *houvera,*	he had had
tiveramos	- *houveramos,*	we had had
tivereis	- *houvereis,*	you had had
tiverão	- *houverão,*	they had had.

Pluperfect.

tinha tido	or *tinha havido,*	I had had
tinhas tido	- *tinhas havido,*	thou hadst had
tinha tido	- *tinha havido,*	he had had
tinhamos tido	- *tinhamos havido,*	we had had
tinheis tido	- *tinheis havido,*	you had had
tinhão tido	- *tinhão havido,*	they had had.

Future.

terei	or *haverei,*	I shall have
terás	- *haverás,*	thou shalt have
terá	- *haverá,*	he shall have
teremos	- *haveremos,*	we shall have
tereis	- *havereis,*	you shall have
terão	- *haverão,*	they shall have.

Compound Future anterior.

hei de ter	or *hei de haver,*	
has de ter	- *has de haver,*	
ha de ter	- *ha de haver,*	I shall (must, will)
havemos de ter	- *havemos de haver,*	have.
haveis de ter	- *haveis de haver,*	
hão de ter	- *hão de haver,*	

Future past.

terei tido	or *terei havido,*	I shall have had
terás tido	- *terás havido,*	thou shalt have had
terá tido	- *terá havido,*	he shall have had
teremos tido	- *teremos havido,*	we shall have had
tereis tido	- *tereis havido,*	you shall have had
terão tido	- *terão havido,*	they shall have had.

Conditional.

teria	or *haveria,*	I should have
terias	- *haverias,*	thou shouldst have
teria	- *haveria,*	he should have
teríamos	- *haveriamos,*	we should have
terieis	- *haverieis,*	you should have
terião	- *haverião,*	they should have.

Conditional past.

teria tido	or *teria havido,*	
terias tido	- *terias havido,*	
teria tido	- *teria havido,*	I should have had.
teriamos tido	- *teriamos havido,*	
terieis tido	- *terieis havido,*	
terião tido	- *terião havido,*	

Subjunctive Mood.

Present.

que tenha	or *haja,*	that I may have
tenhas	- *hajas,*	that thou mayest have
tenha	- *haja,*	that he may have
tenhamos	- *hajamos,*	that we may have
tenhais	- *hajais,*	that you may have
tenhão	- *hajão,*	that they may have.

Imperfect.

que	tivéra	or	houvéra,	that I might have
	tivéras	-	houvéras,	that thou mightst have
	tivéra	-	houvéra,	that he might have
	tivéramos	-	houvéramos,	that we might have
	tivéreis	-	houvéreis,	that you might have
	tivérão	-	houvérão,	that they might have.

Past definite.

que	tivesse	or	houvesse,	that I may have had
	tivesses	-	houvesses,	that thou mayest have had
	tivesse	-	houvesse,	that he may have had
	tivessemos	-	houvessemos,	that we may have had
	tivesseis	-	houvesseis,	that you may have had
	tivéssem	-	houvessem,	that they may have had.

Past indefinite.

que	tenha tido	or	tenha havido,	that I may have had
	tenhas tido	-	tenhas havido,	that thou mayest have had
	tenha tido	-	tenha havido,	that he may have had
	tenhamos tido	-	tenhamos havido,	that we may have had
	tenhais tido	-	tenhais havido,	that you may have had
	tenhão tido	-	tenhão havido,	that they may have had.

Pluperfect.

que	tivesse tido	or	tivesse havido,	that I might have had
	tivesses tido	-	tivesses havido,	that thou mightst have had
	tivesse tido	-	tivesse havido	that he might have had
	tivessemos tido	-	tivessemos havido,	that we might have had
	tivesseis tido	-	tivesseis havido,	that you might have had
	tivessem tido!	-	tivessem havido,	that they might have had.

Simple Future.

quando eu	tiver	or	eu houver,	when I shall have
	tu tiveres	-	tu houveres,	when thou shalt have
	elle tiver	-	elle houver,	when he shall have
	nos tivermos	-	nos houvermos	when we shall have
	vos tiverdes	-	vos houverdes,	when you shall have
	elles tiverem	-	elles houverem,	when they shall have.

Compound Future.

que haja de ter   or *haja de haver,*   that I shall have
   hajas de ter   - *hajas de haver,*   that thou shalt have
   haja de ter   - *haja de haver,*   that he shall have
   hajamos de ter - *hajamos de haver,* that we shall have
   hajais de ter   - *hajais de haver,* that you shall have
   hajão de ter   - *hajão de haver,* that they shall have.

Future past.

quando (se)

 eu tiver tido   or *tiver havido,*   when I shall have had
 ti tiveres tido   - *tiveres havido,*   when thou shalt have had
 elle tiver tido   - *tiver havido,*   when he shall have had
 nos tivermos tido - *tivermos havido,* when we shall have had
 vos tiverdes tido - *tiverdes havido,* when you shall have had
 elles tiverem tido - *tiverem havido,* when they shall have had.

Imperative.

First Person: wanting.

tem tu   or *hajas tu,*   have thou
tenha elle   - *haja elle (ella),*   let him (her) have
tenhamos nós - *hajamos nós,*   let us have
tende vós   - *havei vós,*   have ye
tenhão elles   -- *hajão elles (ellas),* let them have.

Obs. All Verbs composed of *ter,* are conjugated like it, as: *conter, deter, manter, obter, reter* etc.

2.

Examples.

Tenho pão [1]. Tens carne [2]. Elle tem vinho [3]. Tinhamos meixas [4]. Eu tivea morangos [5]. Elle teve uma laranja [6]. Tivemos framboezas [7]. Elles tiverão figos [8]. Hei de ter groselhas [9]. Meu irmão [10] ha de ter nozes [11]. Minhas irmãas [12] hão de ter nesperas [13]. Eu teria vacca [14]. Meu amigo [15] teria vitella [16]. Tereis assado [17]. Elles terião presunto [18]. Tenha elle pastel [19]. Tenhão elles ovos [20]. Tenhamos bolo [21]. Tende vós salada[22]. Que eu tivesse pimenta[23]. Que tu tivesses vinagre[24]. Que elle tivesse azeite[25]. Que nós tivessemos mostarda[26]. Que vós tivesseis assucar[27]. Que elles tivessem especiarias[28].

1 bread. 2 meat. 3 wine. 4 plum. 5 strawberries. 6 orange. 7 raspberry. 8 fig. 9 gooseberry. 10 brother. 11 nut. 12 sister. 13 medlar. 14 beef. 15 friend. 16 veal. 17 the roastmeat. 18 ham. 19. pie. 20 egg. 21 cake. 22 salad. 23 pepper. 24 vinegar. 25 oil. 26 mustard. 27 sugar. 28 spice.

3.

Exercises.

I have beer[1]. Thou hast fruit[2]. He has apples[3]. We have a pear[4]. You have peaches[5]. They have cherries[6]. I had grapes[7]. Thou hadst almonds[8]. He had mulberries[9]. We had an apricot[10]. You had cheese[11]. They had milk[12]. I shall have haselnuts[13]. My brother will have butter[14]. We shall have chesnuts[15]. You will have a lemon[16]. Our gardener[17] will have celery[18]. I would have cake. Thou wouldst have salad. He would have onions[19]. Our game keeper[20] would have venison[21]. We would have sour cherries[22]. You would have raisins[23]. Our cooks[24] would have olives[25]. That our friends[26] have a rosetree[27]. That we have a myrtle[28]. That you have an apricot-tree[29]. That our sisters have a bouquet[30]. That I had cream[31]. That thou hadst salt[32]. That he had coffee[33]. That we had tea[34]. That she had chocolate[35]. Have courage[36]. He may have a book[37]. Let us have patience[38]. Have a watermelon[39]. Let them have a melon[40].

1 cerveja. 2 fruta. 3 maçãa. 4 pera. 5 pecego. 6 cereja. 7 uva. 8 amendoa. 9 amora. 10 albricoque (damasco). 11 queijo. 12 leite. 13 avelãa. 14 manteiga. 15 castanha. 16 limão. 17 jardineiro. 18 aipo. 19 cebola. 20 caçador. 21 caça. 22 ginjas. 23 passas, passas de uva. 24 cozinheira. 25 azeitona. 26 amiga. 27 roseira. 28 murta. 29 damasqueiro. 30 ramalhete. 31 nata. 32 sal. 33 café. 34 chá. 35 chocolate. 36 corragem, animo. 37 livro. 38 paciencia. 39 melancia, balancia. 40 melão.

4.

Examples.

Tenho por ventura [1] uma faca [2]? Tens tu um garfo [3]? Tendes vós guardanapos [4]? Tem elles uma toalha [5]? Tinha eu um prato [6]? Tem ella um copo [7]? Temos nós copos? Tendes vós ouro [8]? Tem elles prata [9]? Tinha eu uma colher [10]? Tinhamos nós uma garrafa [11]? Tinhão elles ferro [12]? Tive eu aça [13]? Tivestes vós chumbo [14]? Terei eu papel [15]? Terás tu pennas [16]? Vosso amigo terá a seu canivete [17]? Teremos nós livros? Tereis vós tinta [18]? Suas irmãas, terão uma casa [19]? Teria eu uma flor [20]? Terieis vós um jardim [21]?

1 by accident. 2 knife. 3 fork. 4 table napkin. 5 towel. 6 plate. 7 glass. 8 gold. 9 silver. 10 spoon. 11 decanter. 12 iron. 13 steel. 14 lead. 15 paper. 16 pens. 17 penknife. 18 ink. 19 house. 20 flower. 21 garden.

5.

Exercises.

Have I by accident a chamber [1]? Hast thou a castle [2]? Has he a tree [3]? Have we money [4]? Are you (have you) thirsty [5]? Have the friends a sword? Had I an opportunity [6]? Hadst thou a razor [7]? Had you a horse [8]? Had you permission [9]? Would I have a tankard [10]? Would she have a cat [11]? Would we have a goat [12]? Would you have a cow [13]? Would they have an ox [14]? Would I have had a mule [15]? Wouldst thou have had a dog [16]?

1 quarto. 2 castello. 3 arvore. 4 dinheiro. 5 sede. 6 occasião. 7 navalha. 8 cavallo. 9 licença. 10 cantaro. 11 gato (gata). 12 cabra. 13 vacca. 14 boi. 15 burro. 16 cão.

.

6.

Conjugation of the Verbs ser and estar, to be.

Infinitive Mood.

Present.	*ser*	or *estar,*	to be
Past.	*ter sido*	- *ter estado,*	to have been.
Gerund.	*sendo*	- *estando,*	being.
Participles.	*sido, sida*	- *estado, estada,*	been.

Indicative Mood.

Present.

eu sou	or *estou,*	I am
tu es	- *estás,*	thou art
elle (ella) he	- *está,*	he (she) is
nós somos	- *estámos,*	we are
vós sois	- *estáis,*	you are
elles (ellas) são	- *estão,*	they are.

Imperfect.

éra	- *estáva,*	I was
eras	- *estavas,*	thou wast
era	- *estava,*	he was
éramos	- *estávamos.*	we were
éreis	- *estaveis,*	you were
érão	- *estávão,*	they were.

Past definite.

fui	or *estive,*	I have been
foste	- *estivéste,*	thou hast been
foi	- *esteve,*	he has been
fomos	- *estivémos,*	we have been
fostes	- *estivestes,*	you have been
forão	- *estivérão,*	they have been.

Past indefinite.

tenho sido	or *tenho estado,*	I have been
tens sido	- *tens estado,*	thou hast been

tem sido	or *tem estado,*	he has been
temos sido	- *temos estado,*	we have been
tendes sido	- *tendes estado,*	you have been
tem sido	- *tem estado,*	they have been.

Past anterior.

fóra	or *estivéra,*	I had been
foras	- *estiveras,*	thou hadst been
fora	- *estivera,*	he had been
foramos	- *estivéramos,*	we had been
foreis	- *estivereis,*	you had been
forão	- *estiverão,*	they had been.

Pluperfect.

tinha sido	or *tinha estado,*	I had been
tinhas sido	- *tinhas estado,*	thou hadst been
tinha sido	- *tinha estado,*	he had been
tinhamos sido	- *tinhamos estado,*	we had been
tinheis sido	- *tinheis estado,*	you had been
tinhão sido	- *tinhão estado,*	they had been.

Future.

seréi	or *estaréi,*	I shall be
serás	- *estarás,*	thou shalt be
será	- *estará,*	he shall be
seremos	- *estaremos,*	we shall be
sereis	- *estareis,*	you shall be
serão	- *estarão,*	they shall be.

Future anterior.

hei de ser	or *hei de estar,*	I shall be
has de ser	- *has de estar*	thou shalt be
ha de ser	- *ha de estar,*	he shall be
havemos de ser	- *havemos de estar,*	we shall be
haveis de ser	- *haveis de estar,*	you shall be
hão de ser	- *hão de estar,*	they shall be.

Future past.

terei sido	or *terei estado,*	I shall have been
terás sido	- *terás estado,*	thou shalt have been

terá sido	or *terá estado,*	he shall have been
teremos sido	- *teremos estado,*	we shall have been
tereis sido	- *tereis estado,*	you shall have been
terão sido	- *terão estado,*	they shall have been.

Conditional.

sería	or *estaría,*	I should be
serias	- *estarias,*	thou shouldst be
seria	- *estaria,*	he should be
seriamos	- *estariamos,*	we should be
serieis	- *estarieis,*	you should be
serião	- *estarião,*	they should be.

Conditional past.

teria sido	or *teria estado,*	I should have been
terias sido,	- *terias estado,*	thou shouldst have been
teria sido	- *teria estado,*	he should have been
teriamos sido	- *teriamos estado,*	we should have been
terieis sido	- *terieis estado,*	you should have been
terião sido	- *terião estado,*	they should have been.

Subjunctive Mood.

Present.

que seja	or *esteja,*	that I may be
sejas	- *estejas,*	that thou mayest be
seja	- *esteja,*	that he may be
sejamos	- *estejamos,*	that we may be
sejais	- *estejais,*	that you may be
sejão	- *estejão,*	that they may be.

Imperfect.

que fora	or *estivera,*	that I might be
foras	- *estiveras,*	that thou mightst be
fora	- *estivera,*	that he might be
foramos	- *estiveramos*	that we might be
foreis	- *estivereis,*	that you might be
forão	- *estiverão,*	that they might be.

Past definite.

que *fosse*	or *estivesse,*	that I may have been
fosses	- *estivesses,*	that thou mayest have been
fosse	- *estivesse,*	that he may have been
fossemos	- *estivessemos,*	that we may have been
fosseis	- *estivesseis,*	that you may have been
fossem	- *estivessem,*	that they may have been.

Past indefinite.

que *tenha sido*	or *tenha estado,*	that I may have been
tenhas sido	- *tenhas estado,*	that thou mayest have been
tenha sido	- *tenha estado,*	that he may have been
tenhamos sido	- *tenhamos estado,*	that we may have been
tenhais sido	- *tenhais estado,*	that you may have been
tenhão sido	- *tenhão estado,*	that they may have been.

Pluperfect.

que *tivesse sido*	or *tivesse estado,*	that I might have been
tivesses sido	- *tivesses estado.*	that thou mightst have been
tivesse sido	- *tivesse estado,*	that he might have been
tivessemos sido	- *tivessemos estado,*	that we might have been
tivesseis sido	- *tivesseis estado,*	that you might have been
tivessem sido	- *tivessem estado,*	that they might have been.

Simple Future.

que *for*	or *estiver,*	that I shall be
fores	- *estiveres,*	that thou shalt be
for	- *estiver,*	that he shall be
formos	- *estivermos,*	that we shall be
fordes	- *estiverdes,*	that you shall be
forem	- *estiverem,*	that they shall be.

Compound Future.

que *haja de ser*	or *haja de estar,*	that I shall be
hajas de ser	- *hajas de estar,*	
haja de ser	- *haja de estar,*	etc.

hajamos de ser or *hajamos de estar,*		that we shall be
hajais de ser - *hajais de estar,*		etc.
hajão de ser - *hajão de estar,*		

Future past.

tiver sido	or *tiver estado,*	when I shall have been
tiveres sido	- *tiveres estado,*	when thou shalt have been
tiver sido	- *tiver estado,*	when he shall have been
tivermos sido	- *tivermos estado,*	when we shall have been
tiverdes sido	- *tiverdes estado,*	when you shall have been
tiverem sido	- *tiverem estado,*	when they shall have been.

quando (bracketing the six forms above)

Imperative.

sê tu	or *está tu,*	be thou
seja elle	- *esteja elle,*	let him be
sejamos nós	- *estejamos nós,*	let us be
sede vós	- *estai vós,*	be ye.
sejão elles	- *estejão elles,*	let them be.

7.

The Regular Verbs.

Active Verbs.

FIRST CONJUGATION.

Amar, to love.

Infinitive Mood.

Present.	*amar,* to love.
Perfect.	*ter amado,* to have loved.
Gerund.	*amando,* loving.
Participles.	*amado, amada,* loved.

Indicative Mood.

Present.

amo, I love	*amamos,* we love
amas, thou lovest	*amais,* you love
ama, he loves	*amão,* they love.

Imperfect.

amava, I loved	*amávamos,* we loved
amavas, thou lovedst	*amaveis,* you loved
amava, he loved	*amavão,* they loved.

Past definite.

amei, I have loved	*amámos,* we have loved
amaste, thou hast loved	*amastes,* you have loved
amou, he has loved	*amárão,* they have loved.

Past indefinite.

tenho amado, I have loved	*temos amado,* we have loved
tens amado, thou hast loved	*tendes amado,* you have loved
tem amado, he has loved	*tem amado,* they have loved.

Past anterior.

amára, I had loved	*amáramos,* we had loved
amáras, thou hadst loved	*amáreis,* you had loved
amára, he had loved	*amárão,* they had loved.

Pluperfect.

tinha amado, I had loved	*tinhamos amado,* we had loved
tinhas amado, thou hadst loved	*tinheis amado,* you had loved
tinha amado, he had loved	*tinhão amado,* they had loved.

Future.

amarei, I shall love	*amaremos,* we shall love
amarás, thou shalt love	*amareis,* you shall love
amará, he shall love	*amarão,* they shall love.

Future anterior.

hei de amar, I shall love — *havemos de avar*, we shall love
has de amar, thou shalt love — *haveis de amar*, you shall love
ha de amar, he shall love — *hão de amar*, they shall love.

Future past.

terei amado, I shall have loved — *teremos amado*, we shall have loved
terás amado, thou shalt have loved — *tereis amado*, you shall have loved
terá amado, he shall have loved — *terão amado*, they shall have loved.

Conditional.

amaria, I should love — *amariamos*, we should love
amarias, thou shouldst love — *amarieis*, you should love
amaria, he should love — *amarião*, they should love.

Conditional past.

teria amado, I should have loved — *teriamos amado*, we should have loved
terias amado, thou shouldst have loved — *terieis amado*, you should have loved
teria amado, he should have loved — *terião amado*, they should have loved.

Subjunctive Mood.

Present.

que ame, that I may love — *que amemos*, that we may love
ames, that thou mayest love — *ameis*, that you may love
ame, that he may love — *amem*, that they may love.

Imperfect.

que amára, that I might love — *que amáramos*, that we might love
amáras, that thou mightst love — *amáreis*, that you might love
amára, that he might love — *amárão*, that they might love.

Past definite.

que amasse, that I may have loved
amasses, that thou mayest have loved
amasse, that he may have loved

que amassemos, that we may have loved
amasseis, that you may have loved
amassem, that they may have loved.

Past indefinite.

que tenha amado, that I may have loved
tenhas amado, that thou mayest have loved
tenha amado, that he may have loved

que tenhamos amado, that we may have loved
tenhais amado, that you may have loved
tenhão amado, that they may have loved.

Pluperfect.

que tivesse amado, that I might have loved
tivesses amado, that thou mightst have loved
tivesse amado, that he might have loved

que tivessemos amado, that we might have loved
tivesseis amado, that you might have loved
tivessem amado, that they might have loved.

Future.

que amar, when I shall love
amares, when thou shalt love
amar, when he shall love

que amarmos, when we shall love
amardes, when you shall love
amarem, when they shall love.

Compound Future.

que haja de amar, that I shall love
hajas de amar, that thou shalt love
haja de amar, that he shall love

que hajamos de amar, that we shall love
hajais de amar, that you shall love
hajão de amar, that they shall love.

Future past.

que *tiver amado*, when I shall have loved
tiveres amado, when thou shalt have loved
tiver amado, when he shall have loved

que *tivermos amado*, when we shall have loved
tiverdes amado, when you shall have loved
tiverem amado, when they shall have loved.

Imperative.

ama tu, love thou
ama elle, let him love

amemos nós, let us love
amai vós, love ye
amem elles, let them love.

8.

SECOND CONJUGATION.

Receber, to receive.

Infinitive Mood.

Present.   *receber*, to receive.
Past.   *ter recebido*, to have received.
Gerund.   *recebendo*, receiving.
Participles. *recebido, -a*, received.

Indicative Mood.

Present.

eu recebo, I receive
tu recebes, thou receivest
elle recebe, he receives

nós recebemos, we receive
vós recebeis, you receive
elles recebem, they receive.

Imperfect.

recebia, I received
recebias, thou receivedst
recebia, he received

recebiamos, we received
recebieis, you received
recebião, they received.

Past definite.

recebi, I have received
recebeste, thou hast received
recebeo, he has received

recebémos, we have received
recebestes, you have received
receberão, they have received.

Past indefinite.

tenho recebido, I have received
tens recebido, thou hast received
tem recebido, he has received

temos recebido, we have received
tendes recebido, you have rec.
tem recebido, they have received.

Past anterior.

recebera, I had received
receberas, thou hadst received
recebera, he had received

receberamos, we had received
recebereis, you had received
receberão, they had received.

Pluperfect.

tinha recebido, I had received
tinhas recebido, thou hadst rec.
tinha recebido, he had received

tinhamos recebido, we had rec.
tinheis recebido, you had rec.
tinhão recebido, they had rec.

Future.

receberei, I shall receive
receberás, thou shalt receive
receberá, he shall receive

receberemos, we shall receive
recebereis, you shall receive
receberão, they shall receive.

Future anterior.

hei de receber, I shall receive
has de receber, thou shalt rec.
ha de receber, he shall receive

havemos de receber, we shall rec.
haveis de receber, you shall rec.
hão de receber, they shall rec.

Future past.

terei recebido, I shall have received
terás recebido, thou shalt have received
terá recebido, he shall have received

teremos recebido, we shall have received
tereis recebido, you shall have received
terão recebido, they shall have received.

Conditional.

receberia, I should receive
receberias, thou shouldst receive
receberia, he should receive

receberiamos, we should receive
receberieis, you should receive
receberião, they should receive.

Conditional past.

teria recebido, I should have received

terias recebido, thou shouldst have received

teria recebido, he should have received

teriamos recebito, we should have received

terieis recebido, you should have received

terião recibido, they should have received.

Subjunctive Mood.

Present.

que receba, that I may receive
recebas, that thou mayest receive
receba, that he may receive

que recebamos, that we may receive
recebais, that you may receive
recebão, that they may receive.

Imperfect.

que recebéra, that I might receive
receberas, that thou mightst receive
recebéra, that he might receive

que recebéremos, that we might receive
recebéreis, that you might receive
recebérão, that they might receive.

Past definite.

que recebesse, that I may have received
recebesses, that thou mayest have received
recebesse, that he may have received

que recebessemos, that we may have receive
recebesseis, that you may have received
recebessem, that they may have received.

Past indefinite.

que tenha recebido, that I may have received
tenhas recebido, that thou mayest have received
tenha recebido, that he may have received

que tenhamos recebido, that we may have received
tenhais recebido, that you may have received
tenhão recebido, that they may have received.

Pluperfect.

que tivesse recebido, that I might have received
tivesses recebido, that thou mightst have received
tivesse recebido, that he might have received

que tivessemos recebido, that we might have received
tivesseis recebido, that you might have received
tivessem recebido, that they might have received.

Future.

quando receber, when I shall receive
receberes, when thou shalt receive
receber, when he shall receive

quando recebermos, when we shall receive
receberdes, when you shall receive
receberem, when they shall receive.

Compound Future.

que haja de receber, that I shall receive
hajas de receber, that thou shalt receive
haja de receber, that he shall receive

que hajamos de receber, that we shall receive
hajais de receber, that you shall receive
hajão de receber, that they shall receive.

Future past.

quando tiver recebido, when I shall have received
tiveres recebido, when thou shalt have received
tiver recebido, when he shall have received

quando tivermos recebido, when we shall have received
tiverdes recebido, when you shall have received
tiverem recebido, when they shall have received.

Imperative Mood.

recebe tu, receive thou
receba elle, let him receive

recebamos nós, let us receive
recebei vós, receive ye
recebão, let them receive.

9.

THIRD CONJUGATION.

Partir, to divide.

Infinitive Mood.

Present.   *partir*, to divide.
Past.   *ter partido*, to have divided.
Gerund.   *partindo*, dividing.
Participles. *partido, partida*, divided.

Indicative Mood.

Present.

parto, I divide
partes, thou dividest
parte, he divides .

partimos, we divide
partis, you divide
partem, they divide.

Imperfect.

partia, I divided
partias, thou dividedst
partia, he divided

partiamos, we divided
partieis, you divided
partião, they divided.

Past definite.

parti, I have divided
partiste, thou hast divided
partio, he has divided

partimos, we have divided
partistes, you have divided
partirão, they have divided.

Past indefinite.

tenho partido, I have divided	*temos partido*, **we** have divided
tens partido, thou hast divided	*tendes partido*, you have divided
tem partido, he has divided	*tem partido*, they have divided.

Past anterior.

partira, I had divided	*partiramos*, we had divided
partiras, thou hadst divided	*partireis*, you had divided
partira, he had divided	*partirão*, they had divided.

Pluperfect.

tinha, partido, I had divided	*tinhamos partido*, we had divided
tinhas partido, thou hadst divided	*tinheis partido*, you had divided
tinha partido, he had divided.	*tinhão partido*, they had divided.

Future.

partirei, I shall divide	*partiremos*, we shall divide
partirás, thou shalt divide	*partireis*, you shall divide
partirá, he shall divide	*partirão*, they shall divide.

Future anterior.

hei de partir, I shall divide	*havemos de partir*, we shall div.
has de partir, thou shalt divide	*haveis de partir*, you shall divide
ha de partir, he shall divide	*hão de partir*, they shall divide.

Future past.

terei partido, I shall have divided	*teremos partido*, we shall have divided
terás partido, thou shalt have divided	*tereis partido*, you shall have divided
terá partido, he shall have divided	*terão partido*, they shall have divided.

Conditional.

partiria, I should divide
partirias, thou shouldst divide
partiria, he should divide

partiriamos, we should divide
partirieis, you should divide
partirião, they should divide.

Conditional past.

teria partido, I should have divided
terias partido, thou shouldst have divided
teria partido, he should have divided

teriamos partido, we should have divided
terieis partido, you should have divided
terião partido, they should have divided.

Subjunctive Mood.

Present.

que parta, that I may divide

partas, that thou mayest divide
parta, that he may divide

que partamos, that we may divide

partais, that you may divide
partão, that they may divide.

Imperfect.

que partira, that I might divide
partiras, that thou mightst divide
partira, that he might divide

que partiramos, that we might divide
partireis, that you might divide
partirão, that they might divide.

Past definite.

que partisse, that I may have divided
partisses, that thou mayest have divided
partisse, that he may have divided

que partissemos, that we may have devided
partisseis, that you .may have divided
partissem, that they may have divided.

Past indefinite.

que *tenha partido,* that I may
have divided
tenhas partido, that thou
mayest have divided
tenha partido, that he may
have divided

que *tenhamos partido,* that we
may have divided
tenhais partido, that you
may have divided
tenhão partido, that they
may have divided.

Pluperfect.

que *tivesse partido,* that I might
have divided
tivesses partido, that thou
mightst have divided
tivesse partido, that he might
have divided

que *tivessemos partido,* that we
might have divided
tivesseis partido, that you
might have divided
tivessem partido, that they
might have divided.

Future.

quando partir, when I shall
divide
partires, when thou
shalt divide
partir, when he shall
divide

quando partirmos, when we
shall divide
partirdes, when you
shall divide
partirem, when they
shall divide.

Compound future.

que *haja de partir,* that I shall
divide
hajas de partir, that thou
shalt divide
haja de partir, that he shall
divide

que *hajamos de partir,* that we
shall divide
hajais de partir, that you
shall divide
hajão de partir, that they
shall divide.

Future past.

quando *tiver partito,* when I shall have divided
    tiveres partido, when thou shalt have divided
    tiver partido, when he shall have divided
    tivermos partido, when we shall have divided
    tiverdes partido, when you shall have divided
    tiverem partido, when they shall have divided.

Imperative Mood.

parte tu, divide thou   *partamos nós,* let us divide
parta elle, let him divide   *parti vós,* divíde ye
                            partão elles, let them divide.

10.

The Passive Verbs.

The Passive Verb is conjugated in all its tenses by the Auxiliary Verb „*ser*" to be, to become, to which is added the Participle of the Passive Verb, as:

sou amado.   — I am loved
tu es amado   — thou art loved
serei amado   — I shall be loved
eu seria amado — I should be loved.

11.

The Neuter Verbs

are conjugated with the Auxiliary Verb „*ter*" to have, as:

tenho dormido,   — I have slept
tenho cahido,   — I have fallen
eu tenho chegado — I have arrived.

They are otherwise conjugated like the Active Verbs *amar, receber, partir.*

12.

The Reflective Verbs

are conjugated with „*ter*“ and the Pronouns *me*, me — *te*, thee — *se*, it — *nos*, we — *vos*, you.

Lembrar-se, to remember.

Infinitive Mood.

Present.   *lembrar-se,* to remember.
Past.   *ter-se lembrado,* to have remembered.
Gerund.   *lembrando-se,* remembering.
Participle. *lembrado, lembrada,* remembered.

Indicative Mood.

Present.

eu me lembro, I remember

nós nos lembramos, we remember

tu te lembras, thou rememberest

vós vos lembrais, you remember

elle se lembra, he remembers

elles se lembrão, they remember.

Imperfect.

eu me lembrava, I remembered

nós nos lembravamos, we remembered

tu te lembravas, thou rememberedst

vós vos lembraveis, you remembered

elle se lembrava, he remembered

elles se lembravão, they remembered.

Past definite.

eu me lembrei, I have remembered

nós nos lembrámos, we have remembered

tu te lembraste, thou hast remembered

vós vos lembrastes, you have remembered

elle se lembrou, he has remembered.

elles se lembrárão, they have remembered.

Past indefinite.

eu me tenho lembrado, I have remembered

tu te tens lembrado, thou hast remembered

elle se tem lembrado, he has remembered

nós nos temos lembrado, we have remembered

vós vos tendes lembrado, you have remembered

elles se tem lembrado, they have remembered.

Past anterior.

eu me lembrára, I had remembered

tu te lembráras, thou hadst remembered

elle se lembrára, he had remembered

nós nos lembráramos, we had remembered

vós vos lembráreis, you had remembered

elles se lembrárão, they had remembered.

Pluperfect.

eu me tinha lembrado, I had remembered

tu te tinhas lembrado, thou ·hadst remembered

elle se tinha lembrado, he had remembered

nós nos tinhamos lembrado, we had remembered

vós vos tinheis lembrado, you had remembered

e es se tinhão lembrado, they had remembered.

Future.

eu me lembrarei, I shall remember

tu te lembrarás, thou shalt remember

elle se lembrará, he shall remember

nós nos lembraremos, we shall remember

vós vos lembrareis, you shall remember

elles se lembrarão, they shall remember.

Future anterior.

eu me hei de lembrar, I shall remember

tu te has de lembrar, thou shalt remember

elle se ha de lembrar, he shall remember

nós nos havemos de lembrar, we shall remember

vós vos haveis de lembrar, you shall remember

elles se hão de lembrar, they shall remember.

Future past.

eu *me terei lembrado,* I shall have remembered
tu *te terás lembrado,* thou shalt have remembered
elle *se terá lembrado,* he shall have remembered

nós *nos teremos lembrado,* we shall have remembered
vós *vos tereis lembrado,* you shall have remembered
elles *se terão lembrado,* they shall have remembered.

Conditional.

eu *me lembraria,* I should remember
tu *te lembrarias,* thou shouldst remember
elle *se lembraria,* he should remember

nós *nos lembrariamos,* we should remember
vós *vos lembrarieis,* you should remember
elles *se lembrarião,* they should remember.

Conditional past.

eu *me teria lembrado,* I should have remembered
tu *te terias lembrado,* thou shouldst have remembered
elle *se teria lembrado,* he should have remembered

nós *nos teriamos lembrado,* we should have remembered
vós *vos terieis lembrado,* you should have remembered
elles *se terião lembrado,* they should have remembered.

Subjunctive Mood.

Present.

que eu *me lembre,* that I may remember
tu *te lembres,* that thou mayest remember
elle *se lembre,* that he may remember

que nós *nos lembremos,* that we may remember
vós *vos lembreis,* that you may remember
elles *se lembrem,* that they may remember.

Imperfect.

que *eu me lembrasse,* that I might remember
tu te lembrasses, that thou mightst remember
elle se lembrasse, that he might remember

que *nós nos lembrassemos,* that we might remember
vós vos lembrasseis, that you might remember
elles se lembrassem, that they might remember.

Past indefinite.

que *eu me tenha lembrado*
tu te tenhas lembrado
elle se tenha lembrado
nós nos tenhamos lembrado
vós vos tenhais lembrado
elles se tenhão lembrado
} that I may have remembered.

Pluperfect.

que *eu me tivesse lembrado*
tu te tivesses lembrado
elle se tivesse lembrado
nós nos tivessemos lembrado
vós vos tivesseis lembrado
elles se tivessem lembrado
} that I might have remembered.

Future.

quando *eu me lembrar*
tu te lembrares
elle se lembrar
nós nos lembrarmos
vós vos lembrardes
elles se lembrarem
} when I shall remember.

Compound Future.

que *eu me haja de lembrar*
tu te hajas de lembrar
elle se haja de lembrar
nós nos hajamos de lembrar
vós vos hajeis de lembrar
elles se hajão de lembrar
} that I shall remember.

Future past.

quando *eu me tiver lembrado*
    tu te tiveres lembrado
    elle se tiver lembrado
    nós nos tivermos lembrado   } when I shall have remem-
    vós vos tiverdes lembrado   bered.
    elles se tiverem lembrado

Imperative Mood.

lembra-te tu,	remember thou
lembre-se elle,	let him remember
lembremos-nos nós,	let us remember
lembrai-vos vós,	remember ye
lembrem-se elles,	let them remember.

Observ. In all the simple tenses of the Indicative Mood, it is unimportant whether the Pronouns *me, te, se, nos, vos* stand before or after the Verb, and one may therefore say either: *eu me lembro,* or *eu lembro-me, eu me lembrava,* and *eu lembrava-me,* but in, the compound tenses as well as in the Subjunctive and Imperative Mood they must stand before the Verb, as: *eu me tenho lembrado, que eu me lembre, que eu me lembrasse.*

13.

Irregular Verbs.

FIRST CONJUGATION.

1. Dar, to give.*)

Indicative Mood.

Present.

eu dou, I give	*Nós damos,* we give
tu dás, thou givest	*vós dais,* you give
elle dá, he gives	*elles dão,* they give.

---

*) Only the irregular tenses are given, the others are conjugated in the regular manner.

Past definite.

eu dei, I have given	*nós demos,* we have given
tu déste, thou hast given	*vós déstes,* you have given
elle deo, he has given	*elles dérão,* they have given.

Past anterior.

eu dera, I had given	*nós deramos,* we had given
tu deras, thou hadst given	*vós dereis,* you had given
elle dera, he had given	*elles derão,* they had given.

Subjunctive Mood.

Present.

que eu dé, that I may give	*que nós démos,* that we may give
tu dés, that thou mayest give	*vós deis,* that you may give
elle dé, that he may give	*elles dem,* that they may give.

Imperfect.

que eu dera, that I might give	*que nós deramos,* that we might give
tu deras, that thou mightst give	*vós dereis,* that you might give
elle dera, that he might give	*elles derão,* that they might give

Past.

que eu désse, that I may have given	*que nos dessemos,* that we may have given
tu désses, that thou mayest have given	*vós desseis* that you may have given
elle désse, that he may have given	*elles dessem,* that they may have given.

Future.

quando *eu der*, when I shall give

tu deres, when thou shalt give

elle der, when he shall give

quando *nós dermos*, when we shall give

vós derdes, when you shall give

elles derem, when they shall give.

---

2. The Verbs ending in „c a r"

have no other irregularity than that they change the *c* every-time into *qu*, if an *e* follows in the conjugation, as: *ficar*, to remain,

fiquei (not *ficei*), I have remained,

que eu fique (not *fice*), that I may remain;

this irregularity is only maintained for the purpose of keeping the same pronunciation for the Verb throughout, which would otherwise not be the case.

---

3. The Verbs ending in „g a r"

change the *g*, if followed by an *e*, into *gu*, for the sake of Pronunciation.

---

4. The Verbs ending in „i a r"

take an *e* before *i* in all persons of the Indicative Mood, as: *premiar*, to reward,

premeio, premeias, premeia, premeiamos etc.

14.

SECOND CONJUGATION.
5. Dizer, to say.

Indicative Mood.

Present.

eu digo, I say
tu dizes, thou sayest
elle diz, he says

nós dizemos, we say
vós dizeis, you say
elles dizem, they say.

Past definite.

eu disse, I have said
tu disseste, thou hast said
elle disse, he has said

nós dissemos, we have said
vós dissestes, you have said
elles disserão, they have said.

Past anterior.

eu dissera, I had said
tu disseras, thou hadst said
elle dissera, he had said

nós disseramos, we had said
vós disserais, you had said
elles disserão, they had said.

Future.

eu direi, I shall say
tu dirás, thou shalt say
elle dirá, he shall say

nós diremos, we shall say
vós direis, you shall say
elles dirão, they shall say.

Conditional.

eu diria, I would say
tu dirias, thou wouldst say
elle diria, he would say

nós diriamos, we would say
vós dirieis, you would say
elles dirião, they would say.

Subjunctive Mood.

Present.

que eu diga, that I may say
tu digas, that thou mayest say
elle diga, that he may say

que nós digamos, that we may say
vós digais, that you may say
elles digão, that they may say.

Imperfect.

que *eu dissera*, that I might say
  tu disseras, that thou mightst
  say
  elle dissera, that he might
  say

que *nós disseramos*, that we
  might say
  vós disserais, that you
  might say
  elles disserão, that they
  might say.

Past.

que *eu dissesse*, that I may have
  said
  tu dissesses, that thou mayest
  have said
  elle dissesse, that he may
  have said

que *nós dissessemos*, that we may
  have said
  vós dissesseis, that you may
  have said
  elles dissessem, that they
  may have said.

Future.

quando *eu disser*, when I shall
  say
  tu disseres, when thou
  shalt say
  elle disser, when he
  shall say

quando *nós dissermos*, when we
  shall say
  vós disserdes, when you
  shall say
  elles disserem, when they
  shall say.

Imperative Mood.

dize-tu, say thou
diga-elle, let him say

digamos-nós, let us say
dizei-vós, say ye
digão-elles, let them say.

Participle: *dito, dita,* said.

All Verbs composed of *dizer* are conjugated in the same manner, as: *contradizer, desdizer,* etc.

---

6. Fazer, to do, to make.

Indicative Mood.

Present.

eu *faço*, I do   nós *fazemos*, we do
tu *fazes*, thou dost   vós *fazeis*, you do
elle *faz*, he does   elles *fazem*, they do.

Past definite.

eu *fiz*, I have done   nós *fizemos*, we have done
tu *fizeste*, thou hast done   vós *fizestes*, you have done
elle *fez*, he has done   elles *fizerão*, they have done

Pluperfect.

eu *fizera*, I had done   nós *fizeramos*, we had done
tu *fizeras*, thou hadst done   vós *fizereis*, you had done
elle *fizera*, he had done   elles *fizerão*, they had done.

Future.

eu *farei*, I shall do   nós *faremos*, we shall do
tu *farás*, thou shalt do   vós *fareis*, you shall do
elle *fará*, he shall do   elles *farão*, they shall do.

Conditional.

eu *faria*, I would do   nós *fariamos*, we would do
tu *farias*, thou wouldst do   vvs *farieis*, you would do
elle *faria*, he would do   elles *farião*, they would do.

Subjunctive Mood.

Present.

que eu *faça*, that I may do   que nós *façamos*, that we may do
tu *faças*, that thou mayest do   vós *façais*, that you may do
elle *faça*, that he may do   elles *fação*, that they may do.

Imperfect.

que eu *fizera*, that I might do
tu *fizeras*, that thou mightst do
elle *fizera*, that he might do

que nós *fizeramos*, that we might do
vós *fizerais*, that you might do
elles *fizerão*, that they might do.

Perfect.

que eu *fizesse*, that I may have done
tu *fizesses*, that thou mayest have done
elle *fizesse*, that he may have done

que nós *fizessemos*, that we may have done
vós *fizesseis*, that you may have done
elles *fizessem*, that they may have done.

Future.

quando eu *fizer*, when I shall do
tu *fizeres*, when thou shalt do
elle *fizer*, when he shall do

quando nós *fizermos*, when we shall do
vós *fizerdes*, when you shall do
elles *fizerem*, when they shall do.

Imperative Mood.

faze-tu, do thou
faça elle, let him do

façamos-nós, let us do
fazei-vós, do ye
fação elles, let them do.

Participle: *feito, feita,* done.

---

7. Poder, to be able, to can.

Indicative Mood.

Present.

eu *posso*, I can
tu *podes*, thou canst
elle *póde*, he can

nós *podemos*, we can
vós *podeis*, you can
elles *podem*, they can.

Perfect.

eu pude, I have been able
tu pudeste, thou hast been able
elle pode, he has been able

nós pudemos, we have been able
vós pudestes, you have been able
elles puderão, they have been able.

Pluperfect.

eu pudera, I had been able
tu puderas, thou hadst been able
elle pudera, he had been able

nós puderamos, we had been able
vós pudereis, you had been able
elles puderão, they had been able.

Subjunctive Mood.

Present.

que eu possa, that I may be able
tu possas, that thou mayest be able
elle possa, that he may be able

que nós possamos, that we may be able
vós possais, that you may be able
elles possão, that they may be able.

Imperfect.

que eu pudera, that I might be able
tu puderas, that thou mightst be able
elle pudera, that he might be able

que nós puderamos, that we might be able
vós pudereis, that you might be able
elles puderão, that they might be able.

Perfect.

que eu pudesse, that I may have been able
tu pudesses, that thou mayest have been able
elle pudesse, that he may have been able

que nós pudessemos, that we may have been able
vós pudesseis, that you may have been able
elles pudessem, that they may have been able.

Future.

quando eu puder, if I could be able
tu puderes, if thou couldst be able
elle puder, if he could be able

quando nós pudermos, if we could be able
vós puderdes, if you could be able
elles puderem, if they could be able.

---

8. Querer, to wish, to will.

Indicative Mood.

Present.

eu quero, I wish
tu queres, thou wishest
elle quer, he wishes

nós queremos, we wish
vós quereis, you wish
elles querem, they wish.

Perfect.

eu quiz, I have wished
tu quizeste, thou hast wished
elle quiz, he has wished

nós quizemos, we have wished
vós quizestes, you have wished
elles quizerão, they have wished.

Pluperfect.

eu quizera, I had wished
tu quizeras, thou hadst wished
elle quizera, he had wished

nós quizeramos, we had wished
vós quizereis, you had wished
elles quizerão, they had wished.

Subjunctive Mood.

Present.

que eu queira, that I may wish
tu queiras, that thou mayest wish
elle queira, that he may wish

que nós queiramos, that we may wish
vós queirais, that you may wish
elles queirão, that they may wish.

Imperfect.

que eu quizera, that I might wish

tu quizeras, that thou mightst wish

elle quizera, that he might wish

que nós quizeramos, that we might wish

vós quizereis, that you might wish

elles quizerão, that they might wish.

Perfect.

que eu quizesse, that I may have wished

tu quizesses, that thou mayest have wished

elle quizesse, that he may have wished

que nós quizessemos, that we may have wished

vós quizesseis, that you may have wished

elles quizessem, that they may have wished.

Future.

quando eu quizer, when I shall wish

tu quizeres, when thou shalt wish

elle quizer, when he shall wish

quando nós quizermos, when we shall wish

vós quizerdes, when you shall wish

elles quizerem, when they shall wish.

Imperative Mood.

queiras tu, wish thou

queira elle, let him wish

queiramos nós, let us wish

queirais vós, wish ye

queirão elles, let them wish.

O que é que o Sñr. quer? Eu queria fallar com a Senhora sua tia. Ella quiz sahir[1], póde ser que já sahisse. Quizeramos dar-lhe tudo quanto[2] aquelle desgraçado precisasse[3], mas elle preferiu[4] partir, e nunca mais temos ouvido[5] fallar d'elle. Não me queira enfadar[6], Senhor, que basta[7] eu saber que não merece a minha valiosa[8] protecção[9]. Eu quereria

1 to go out. 2 all that. 3 precisar, to require. 4 preferir, to prefer. 5 ouvir, to hear. 6 enfadar, to tire. 7 bastar, to satisfy. 8 valuable. 9 protection.

me incumbir [10] deste negocio, mas témo [11] a lealdade [12] d'esse homem. Faça o Sñr. o que quizer, eu não o estorvo [13].

10 incubir de, to undertake. 11 temer, to fear. 12 the honesty.
13 estorvar, to disturb.

Do you wish to grieve me with this news? On the contrary [1] I wished to please you with it. I wished that you should be glad about [2] the favourable [3] indications [4]. It is necessary that you should really [5] wish the happiness [6] of that family. If we desired the misfortune [7] of those people, we would give them different advice [8]. If that old man had wished to breakfast with us, he would not have gone away an hour ago [9]. Whenever you wish to visit [10] us, pray send [11] a messenger [12]. He would wish to surprise [13] us. Who wishes to buy [14] this ring of me? He who does not wish to work will have nothing to eat [15].

1 pelo contrario. 2 por. 3 favoravel. 4 indicio. 5 realmente. 6 felicidade. 7 o mal. 8 conselho. 9 ha. 10 visitar. 11 mandar. 12 o proprio. 13 sorprenhender. 14 comprar. 15 comer.

---

9. Saber, to know.

Indicative Mood.

Present.

eu sei, I know	*nós sabemos*, we know
tu sabes, thou knowest	*vós sabeis*, you know
elle sabe, he knows	*elles sabem*, they know.

Perfect.

eu soube, I have known	*nós soubemos*, we have known
tu soubeste, thou hast known	*vós soubestes*, you have known
elle soube, he has known	*elles souberão*, they have known.

Pluperfect.

eu soubera, I had known	*nós souberamos*, we had known
tu souberas, thou hadst known	*vós soubereis*, you had known
elle soubera, he had known	*elles souberão*, they had known.

Subjunctive Mood.
Present.

que eu saiba, that I may know
tu saibas, that thou mayest know
elle saiba, that he may know

que nós saibamos, that we may know
vós saibais, that you may know
elles saibão, that they may know.

Imperfect.

que eu soubera, that I might know
tu souberas, that thou mightst know
elle soubera, that he might know

que nós souberamos, that we might know
vós soubereis, that you might know
elles souberão, that they might know.

Future.

quando eu souber, when I shall know
tu souberes, when thou shalt know
elle souber, when he shall know

quando nós soubermos, when we shall know
vós souberdes, when you shall know
elles souberem, when they shall know.

Imperative Mood.

sabe tu, know thou
saiba elle, let him know

saibamos nós, let us know
saibei vós, know ye
saibão elles, let them know.

Já sabe que nunca mais havemos de andar a cavallo por este caminho[1] em quanto elle não estiver concertado? He agora mesmo que estou sabendo. Si eu soubera que foi elle quem apagou a luz! Nada soubemos désse acontecimento[2], aliás[3] não o teriamos deixado ahi. Elle quiz por força[4] que nos

1 the road, way. 2 event. 3 else. 4 absolutely.

soubessemos alguma cousa [5] sobre as circumstancias [6] d'aquelle sujeito [7]. Quando os Senhores souberem tudo, hão de dizer que eu tive razão. Pois saiba que é Vm. só que tem culpa. Eu não sei por que razão o Sñr. não aprecia esta paizagem? [8]

5 something. 6 circumstances. 7 subject. 8 landscape.

If we really [1] knew that our partner would not return [2], we would divide [3] the profit [4]. I have never known anything of it, it is to-day the first time, that I hear talk of such things. I can assure [5] you, that we knew nothing when the bearer [6] of this letter arrived. As soon as we know it for certain [7] we will give you notice. Now Sir, you may know that we are lost and that there is no chance [8] of preventing [9] the downfall [10] of our house.

1 effectivamente. 2 voltar. 3 repartir. 4 o ganho. 5 asseverar.
6 o portador. 7 a certeza. 8 probabilidade. 9 evitar. 10 a queda.

---

10. Tazer, to carry, to fetch, to bring.

Indicative Mood.

Present.

eu trago, I carry	*nós trazemos*, we carry
eu trazes, thou carriest	*vós trazeis*, you carry
elle traz, he carries	*elles trazem*, they carry.

Perfect.

eu trouxe, I have carried	*nós trouxemos*, we have carried
tu trouxeste, thou hast carried	*vós trouxestes*, you have carried
elle trouxe, he has carried	*elles trouxerão*, they have carried.

Pluperfect.

eu trouxera, I had carried	*nós trouxeramos*, we had carried
tu trouxeras, thou hadst carried	*vós trouxéreis*, you had carried
elle trouxera, he had carried	*elles trouxerão*, they had carried.

Future.

eu trarei, I shall carry	*nós traremos*, we shall carry
tu trarás, thou shalt carry	*vós trareis*, you shall carry
elle trará, he shall carry	*elles trarão*, they shall carry.

Conditional.

eu traria, I should carry	*nós trariamos*, we should carry
tu trarias, thou shouldst carry	*vós trarieis*, you should carry
elle traria, he should carry	*elles trarião*, they should carry.

Subjunctive Mood.

Present.

que eu traga, that I may carry	*que nós tragamos*, that we may carry
tu tragas, that thou mayest carry	*vós tragais*, that you may carry
elle traga, that he may carry	*elles tragão*, that they may carry.

Imperfect.

que eu trouxera, that I might carry	*que nós trouxeramos*, that we might carry
tu trouxeras, that thou mightst carry	*vós trouxereis*, that you might carry
elle trouxera, that he might carry	*elles trouxerão*, that they might carry.

Perfect.

que eu trouxesse, that I may have carried	*que nós trouxessemos*, that we may have carried
tu trouxesses, that thou mayest have carried	*vós trouxesseis*, that you may have carried
elle trouxesse, that he may have carried	*elles trouxessem*, that they may have carried.

Future.

quando eu trouxer, when I shall carry	*quando nós trouxermos*, when we shall carry
tu trouxeres, when thou shalt carry	*vós trouxerdes*, when you shall carry
elle trouxer, when he shall carry	*elles trouxerem*, when they shall carry.

Imperative Mood.

traze tu, carry thou	*tragamos*, let us carry
traga elle, let him carry	*trazei vós*, carry ye
	tragão elles, let them carry.

Tragão seis cópos de agua d'ahi! Traz fôgo, rapaz! Quando os negros trouxerem os barris havemos de enchê-los[1]. Si nos não trouxeramos tantos mantimentos[2] para cá, havião de morrer de fóme. Não quizerão os colonos que os seus patricios lhes trouxessem algumas plantas e sementes[3] de sua terra? Quer que lhes tragamos d'aquellas frutas que nós compramos áquelles fazendeiros[4]? Agora me dá essa caixa[5], depois me trará tudo quanto se acha n'aquelles dois aposentos[6]. Então não trouxerão nada para mim? Sempre trazemos alguma cousa posto que[7] totalmente insignificante[8].

1 encher, to fill. 2 provisions. 3 the seed. 4 proprietor of an estate. 5 the case. 6 the room. 7 although. 8 insignificant.

Do not allow[1] your slave[2] to carry this basket[3], for it is too heavy[4] for her. We have brought every thing we found in that wood[5]. Do you not wish to hear the news[6] which the traveller[7] brings? The papers[8] last[9] year 'brought bad[10] news about the plantations of that province. There is[11] the postman[12], what will he bring? If you had brought money, you would not have failed[13] to come yesterday. As soon as our enemies will bring us the documents[14] demanded[15], we

1 admittir. 2 escrava. 3 o cesto. 4 pesado. 5 o mato. 6 a nova. 7 o viajante. 8 a gazeta. 9 passado. 10 triste. 11 eis. 12 cartevio. 13 deixar. 14 o documento. 15 exigir.

shall be conquerors[16]. Do you wish me to bring them? You may bring them. Bring a light, nigro[17]! Bring something to eat, we are hungry. I am bringing it.

16 vencedor. 17 o negro.

---

11. Ver, to see.

Indicative Mood.

Present.

eu vejo, I see
tu vês, thou seest
elle vê, he sees

nós vemos, we see
vós vedes, you see
elles vêm, they see.

Imperfect.

eu vi, I have seen
tu viste, thou hast seen
elle vio, he has seen

nós vimos, we have seen
vós vistes, you have seen
elles virão, they have seen.

Pluperfect.

eu vira, I had seen
tu viras, thou hadst seen
elle vira, he had seen

nós viramos, we had seen
vós vireis, you had seen
elles virão, they had seen.

Subjunctive Mood.

Present.

que eu veja, that I may see
tu vejas, that thou mayest see
elle veja, that he may see

que nós vejamos, that we may see
vós vejais, that you may see
elles vejão, that they may see.

Imperfect.

que eu vira, that I might see
tu viras, that thou mightst see
elle vira, that he might see

que nós viramos, that we might see
vós virais, that you might see
elles virem, that they might see.

Perfect.

que eu visse, that I may have seen
tu visses, that thou mayest have seen
elle visse, that he may have seen

que nós vissemos, that we may have seen
vós visseis, that you may have seen
elles vissem, that they may have seen.

Future.

quando eu vir, when I shall see
tu vires, when thou shalt see
elle vir, when he shall see

quando nós virmos, when we shall see
vós virdes, when you shall see
elles virem, when they shall see.

Imperative Mood.

vé tu, see
veja elle, let him see

vejamos nós, let us see
vede vós, see ye
vejão elles, let them see.

Participle: *visto, vista*, seen.

The Verbs composed of *ver*, are conjugated in the same manner, as: *prever, rever, antever.*

Nisto eu não vejo nada de máo. Não vé o Senhor que elle não póde. Nunca vimos homens mais assiduos [1] que esses estrangeiros. Si vissem tudo o que se faz n'aquellas casas, estarião admirados [2]. Veja quanto é do mez [3]. Não vio que elles não querem se dar [4] com nosco? E' porque não vêm que seus parentes nos procurão [5]. Logo que virmos mais docilidade [6] da parte d'elles, não seremos mais contra elles. Não viamos todos os dias gente chegar ás nossas praias [7]? Os Senhores hão de vér que todos os seus esforços serão baldados [8].

1 industrious. 2 astonished. 3 what date? 4 *dar-se com alguem* to be acquainted with one. 5 to seek. 6 indulgence. 7 the strand. 8 to mediate.

Hontem vimos no theatro gente que não tem idéa⁹ do que se chama decencia¹⁰. Ora, vejão como elle finge¹¹ não ver-nos.

9 the idea. 10 decency. 11 *fingir*, to do as if.

Will you see, how false¹ this news² will be? Well, let us see. When you see the prettily cultivated³ mountains⁴ of this land, you will find them beautiful⁵. If you had at least⁶ seen two or three of the chief⁷ places⁸ of our country, you could form an idea of the regularity⁹, with which our over-seers¹⁰ manage¹¹ the cleansing of our streets¹². After having seen this, we did not wish to see the rest¹³.

1 falso. 2 o boato. 3 cultivar. 4 outeiro. 5 encantador. 6 ao menos. 7 importante. 8 a praça. 9 regularidade. 10 o empregado. 11 observar. 12 limpeza das ruas. 13 o resto.

---

12. Perder, to lose.

The irregularity of this Verb consists in the following tenses changing the *d* into *c*.

Indicative Mood.

Present.

perco, I lose	*perdemos*, we lose
perdes, thou losest	*perdeis*, you lose
perde, he loses	*perdem*, they lose.

Subjunctive Mood.

Present.

que eu perca, that I may lose	*que nós percamos*, that we may lose
tu percas, that thou mayest lose	*vós percais*, that you may lose
elle perca, that he may lose	*elles percão*, that they may lose.

8*

Imperative Mood.

perde tu, lose thou	*percamos nós*, let us lose
perca elle, let him lose	*perdei vós*, lose ye
	percão elles, let them lose.

---

13. Valer, to be worth,

changes *l* into *lh*, in the following tenses.

Indicative Mood.

Present.

eu valho, I am worth	*nós valemos*
tu vales } regular	*vós valeis* } regular.
elle vale	*elles valem*

Subjunctive Mood.

Present.

que eu valha, that I may be worth	*que nos valhamos*, that we may be worth
tu valhas, that thou mayest be worth	*vos valhais*, that you may be worth
elle valha, that he may be worth	*elles valhão*, that they may be worth.

Imperative Mood.

vale tu, be thou worth	*valhamos*, let us be worth
valha elle, let him be worth	*valei vós*, be ye worth
	valhão elles, let them be worth.

---

14. Ler, to read.

Indicative Mood.

Present.

eu leio, I read	*nós lemos*, we read
tu lês, thou readest	*vós ledes*, you read
elle lê, he reads	*elles lêm*, they read.

Subjunctive Mood.

Present.

que eu léia, that I may read *que nós léiamos*, that we may read
tu léias, that thou mayest read
elle léia, that he may read

vós léiais, that you may read
elles léião, that they may read.

Imperative Mood.

lé tu, read thou
léia elle, let him read

léiamos, let us read
lede vós, read ye
léião elles, let them read.

The Verb *crer* to believe, is conjugated in the same manner.

---

15. The Verbs ending in „ger"

change *g* into *j* in all persons when it is followed by *o* or *a*, for the sake of pronunciation. As; *eleger*, to elect; *elejo*, *que eu eleja*, etc.

Examples.

Não hei de jogar mais porque perco sempre. Ainda que esse mísero[1] jogador[2] perca tudo, nem por isso[3] não deixa de apparecer[4] cá. Neste negocio perdemos mais de quinhentos mil reis. Infelizmente[5] sou eu quem perdeu tres vezes mais que o meu socio. Quanto vale (how much is to cost) seu cavallo? Quanto custou a mula? Custou-me cento e cincoenta mil reis.

1 miserable. 2 gamester. 3 *nem por isso*, yet. 4 appear. 5 unfortunately.

Exercises.

It seems to me that he has lost his reason[1]. It is I who lose by his imprudence[2]. Be careful[3] that[4] you do

1 juizo. 2 imprudencia. 3 tomar sentido. 4 para que.

not lose the confidence[5] in[6] yourself. A good[7] conscience[8] is worth more than riches[9], gained[10] by[11] immoral[12] means. I doubt, that the work is worth more than yours. Do not allow your daughters to read books which do not contain moral[13] principles[14]. It seems[15] to me that you are reading novels[16] translated[17] from[18] the french. I only read at night[19]. I find, that the boy reads very well.

> 5 confiança. 6 em. 7 tranquillo. 8 consciencia. 9 riqueza. 10 adquerir. 11 por. 12 immoral. 13 moral. 14 principio. 15 parecer. 16 o romance. 17 traduzir. 18 de. 19 de noite.

15.

THIRD CONJUGATION.

16. Ir, to go.

Indicative Mood.

Present.

eu vou, I go	*nós vamos*, we go
tu vas, thou goest	*vós ides*, you go
elle vai, he goes	*elles vão*, they go.

Imperfect.

eu hia, I went	*nós hiamos*, we went
tu hias, thou wentest	*vós hieis*, you went
elle hia, he went	*elles hião*, they went.

Perfect.

eu fui, I have gone (like the Perfect of *ser* to be).

Pluperfect.

eu fora, I had gone (like the Pluperfect of *ser*).

Subjunctive Mood.

Present.

que eu vá, that I may go	*que nós vámos*, that we may go
tu vás, that thou mayest go	*vós vades*, that you may go
elle vá, that he may go	*elles vão*, that they may go.

Imperfect.

que eu fora, that I might go
tu foras, that thou mightest go
elle fora, that he might go

que nós foramos, that we might go
vós foreis, that you might go
elles forão, that they might go.

Perfect.

que eu fosse, that I might have gone (like „*ser*").

Future.

quando eu for, when I shall go (like „*ser*").

Imperative Mood.

vai tu, go thou
vá elle, let him go

vamos, let us go
ide vós, go ye
vão elles, let them go.

Examples.

Ido, gone. *Ir-se embora,* to go away.

Quer que vamos vêr o jardim que hontem comprámos. Se eu fosse tão de vagar como o Sñr., não alcançava hoje a cidade. Quando formos outra vez [1], iremos mais de pressa [2]. O bom velho hia todos os dias ver o túmulo [3] da finada [4] mulher. Para onde quer que elle vá, nunca deixa de levar comsigo [5] o retrato [6] do seu único [7] amigo. Vamos ver se agora poderemos concluir [8] esse negocio. Não querem os Senhores ir vêr o célebre [9] hóspede? [10] Imos ouvir a grande cantora [11] que chegou ha poucos dias dos Estados-Unidos [12]. Eu nunca tenho ido ao theatro sem levar comigo toda a minha familia.

1 again. 2 quick. 3 the grave. 4 deceased. 5 with him. 6 the picture. 7 only. 8 to finish. 9 celebrated. 10 guest. 11 singer. 12 the United States.

Se elles não forem-se embora já e já[13], mandamos chamar[14] a policia[15]. Va para fora[16], malcriado[17], e não volte mais para cá. Eu já vou-me embora. Vái de pressa, filho, senão[18] não o alcanças mais. Nos iriamos embora ainda[19] hoje, si não receassemos[20] o descontentamento[21] do nosso amo. Fui-me embora sem mais[22] ceremonia. Elles já se tinhão ido embora quando chegárão os convidados[23]. Vai-te embora, amigo, tu não me convences. Si não formos embora hoje, não iremos nunca.

13 immediately. 14 to call. 15 the police. 16 go away. 17 ill-bred. 18 if not. 19 yet. 20 *recear*, to fear. 21 discontent. 22 *sem mais*, without further. 23 *convidar*, to invite.

---

17. Vir, to come.

Indicative Mood.

Present.

eu venho, I come	*nós vimos*, we come
tu vens, thou comest	*vós vindes*, you come
elle vem, he comes	*elles vem*, they come.

Imperfect.

eu vinha, I came	*nós vinhamos*, we came
tu vinhas, thou camest	*vós vinheis*, you came
elle vinha, he came	*elles vinhão*, they came.

Perfect.

eu vim, I have come	*nós viemos*, we have come
tu vieste, thou hast come	*vós viestes*, you have come
elle veio, he has come	*elles vierão*, they have come.

Pluperfect.

eu viera, I had come	*nós vieramos*, we had come
tu vieras, thou hadst come	*vós viereis*, you had come
elle viera, he had come	*elles vierão*, they had come.

Subjunctive Mood.

Present.

que eu venha, that I may come
tu venhas, that thou mayest come
elle venha, that he may come

que nós venhamos, that we may come
vós venhais, that you may come
elles venhão, that they may come.

Imperfect.

que eu viera, that I might come
tu vieras, that thou mightest come
elle viera, that he might come

que nós vieramos, that we might come
vós viereis, that you might come
elles vierão, that they might come.

Perfect.

que eu viesse, that I may have come
tu viesses, that thou mayest have come
elle viesse, that he may have come

que nós viessemos, that we may have come
vós viesseis, that you may have come
elles viessem, that they may have come.

Future.

quando eu vier, when I shall come
tu vieres, when thou shalt come
elle vier, when he shall come

quando nós viermos, when we shall come
vós vierdes, when you shall come
elles vierem, when they shall come.

Imperative Mood.

vem tu, come
venha elle, let him come

venhamos, let us come
vinde vos, come ye
venhão elles, let them come.

Participle: *vindo, vinda*, come.

In the same manner are conjugated the compound verbs:
convir, *intervir*, *subrevir*, *prevenir*, to prevent, to warn.

Pres. *Eu previno* — *nós prevenimos*
tu prevines — *vós prevenis*
elle previne — *elles previnem.*

Conj. *Que eu previna*, etc.

Examples.

, Os Portuguezes quando vierão para o Brazil puzerão-se[1]
logo a maltratar[2] os indígenas[3]. Quem he que veio? E' o
nosso velho Bahiano[4] que acaba de vir das provincias do
norte[5]. Vim para lhe dizer, Sñr., que não lhe posso acompanhar[6] para a fazenda[7] d'aquelle Inglez. Queríamos muito
que seus filhos viessem passar[8] as férias[9] com nosco na roça[10].
Quando o tropeiro[11] viér do Sul[12] elle traz para nós cavallos
que nunca forão montados[13]. Tendo vindo tantos colonos da
Allemanha para o Brazil, o governo[14] mandou logo medir[15]
o terreno. Os colonos vindos de Portugal não querião plantar.

1 to begin. 2 ill-treat. 3 natives. 4 inhab. of Bahia. 5 the north.
6 to accompany. 7 country estate. 8 pass. 9 holydays. 10
woodlands. 11 the troop (of cattle). 12 the south. 13 mount.
14 the government. 15 to survey.

Exercises.

When does your teacher[1] come, who was with you yesterday? Will you let me know when he comes? He cannot come these next few days. I wished he would come to
me[2] before the end[3] of this week. As soon as our guests had
come, we went with them to our great estate, where indian
tea[4] is grown[5]. As soon as your relations[6] come, we will
take a journey with them to that great waterfall[7]. Where do
these travellers come from? If you had not come to day,
I should have believed you to be ill[8]. Tell your cousins that
they may come to see us.

1 professor, mestre. 2 me ver. 3 fim. 4 chá da India. 5 cul-
tivar. 6 o parente. 7 a cachoeira. 8 advecer.

18. Pedir, to request,

chauges *d* in *ç* in the following persons.

Indicative Mood.

Present.

eu peço, I request (the other persons are regular: *pedes, pede*, etc.).

Subjunctive Mood.

Present.

que eu peça, that I may request
   tu peças, that thou mayest request
   elle peça, that he may request

que nós peçamos, that we may request
   vós peçais, that you may request
   elles peção, that they may request.

Imperative Mood.

pede tu, request
peça elle, let him request

peçamos nos, let us request
pedi vós, request ye
peção elles, let them request.

„*Medir*" to mesure, is conjugated in the same manner.

---

19. Rir, to laugh.

Indicative Mood.

Present.

eu rio, I laugh
tu ris, thou laughest
elle ri, he laughs

nós rimos, we laugh
vós rides, you laugh
elles rim, they laugh.

Subjunctive Mood.

Present.

que eu ria, that I may laugh
tu rias, that thou mayest laugh
elle ria, that he may laugh

que nós riamos, that we may laugh
vós riais, that you may laugh
elles rião, that they may laugh.

Imperative Mood.

ri tu, laugh
ria elle, let him laugh

riamos, let us laugh
ride vós, laugh ye
rião elles, let them laugh.

---

20. The Verbs ending in „ g i r "

change the *g* into *j* in all persons where *g* is followed by *o* or *a.*

---

21. The Verbs ending in „ u z i r "

drop the final *e* in the third person Singular of the Present, as: *conduz* (not *conduze*), *induz* (not *induze*).

Conduzir, to conduct.

Pres. *Eu conduzo, tu conduzes, elle conduz, nós conduzimos*, etc., in the same manner: *luzir*, to light.

---

22. The Verbs ending in „ h i r "

change *hi* into *i* in the following persons.

sahir, to go out.

Indicative Mood.

Present.

eu saio, I go out (the others are regular: *sahes, sahe, sahi-mos*, etc.).

Subjunctive Mood.

Present.

que eu saia, that I may go out

tu saias, that thou mayest go out

elle saia, that he may go out

que nós saiamos, that we may go out

vós saiais, that you may go out

elles saião, that they may go out.

Imperative Mood.

sahe tu, go out

saia elle, let him go out

saiamos nós, let us go out

sahi vós, go ye out

saião elles, let them go out.

In the same manner are conjugated:

cahir, to fall; *trahir*, to betray; *decahir*, to decay; *contrahir*, to contract.

---

23. Subir, to mount,

changes *u* into *o*, in the second person Singular, third person Singular and Plural of the Present, and in the second person of the Imperative, as:

Pres. *Eu subo, tu sóbes, elle sóbe, nós subímos, vós sobis, elles sobém.*

Conj. *Que eu suba.*   Imper. *sobe tu, subí vos.*

In the same manner are conjugated:

acudir,	to assist		*fugir,*	to fly
bulir,	to move		*engulir,*	to swallow
construir,	to construct ·		*sacudir,*	to shake
cuspir,	to spit		*tussir,*	to cough
destruir,	to destroy		*cubrir,*	to cover.

Examples.

Eu peço lhe licença[1] para acompanhar seu mano. Nós não desejamos que elles oução a nossa conversa[2]. Rirão-se todos quando vírão o modo[3] por que o fazendeiro castigou o seu feitor[4]. Veja como elle conduz o preso[5] que finge não poder andar. Saia para fóra, homem! não gosto de mentirosos[6]. Elle diz que subamos e escada[7] da mão esquerda. Então não me acódes n'esta penúria?[8] Hoje o Sñr. não sahe mais? nem de noite? Não bula nestes papeis, que não são meus. Mandem que conduzão para cá o accusado[9]. Construamos ahi[10] um edificio que seja digno[11] de nossa arte[12]. Ouça homem! não foi elle quem lhe contou isso. Querem que não riamos d'elle, e todavía[13] são ridiculas[14] suas pretenções[15]. Não cospe no chão[16], menino! é muito máo costume. Não me peça isto, que não lhe posso conceder. Eu não ouvi nada dizer a este respeito. Veja, que as formigas[17] não destruão[18] os legumes[19]. O que eu desejo é que elle não fuja d'elle. Hei de impedir[20] que elles engulão as píllulas[21] que Vm. lhes destinou. Cubra-se bem, para suar bastante. Esses meninos não ouvem, parecem surdos[22]. Desejo muito que não caia doente outra vez.

1 licence. 2 conversation. 3 the manner. 4 the steward. 5 the prisoner. 6 liar. 7 the staircase. 8 the want. 9 *accusar,* to accuse. 10 there. 11 worthy. 12 art. 13 nevertheless, yet. 14 ridiculous. 15 pretention. 16 the soil. 17 ant. 18 *destruir,* to destroy. 19 vegetables. 20 to impede. 21 pill. 22 deaf.

Exercises.

Why do you not hear! Let us go up at once, or we shall not meet[1], him. He is not here, he is already gone out. You must lead[2] him, he is too weak to walk. If you had heard everything, he said of you. These fools laughed at us, because they knew not our intentions. If he asks us to go into the garden, we shall go. I hear nothing, the children make to much noise[3]. Why do you fly from us? You destroy all my plans.

1 encontrar. 2 guiar. 3 o barulho.

---

24. Mentir, to lie,

changes *e* into *i* in the following persons.

Indicative Mood.

Present.

eu minto, I lie (*tu mentes, elle mente*).

Subjunctive Mood.

Present.

que eu minta, that I may lie *tu mintas*, that thou mayest lie *elle minta*, that he may lie	*que nós mintamos*, that we may lie *vós minais*, that you may lie *elles mintão*, that they may lie.

Imperative Mood.

mente tu, lie *minta elle*, let him lie	*mintamos nós*, let us lie *menti vós*, lie ye *mintão elles*, let them lie.

The same irregularities occur in *sentir*, to feel — *servir*, to serve — *ferir*, to wound.

---

25. Dormir, to sleep.

This Verb changes *e* into *u* in all persons, in which *mentir* changes the *e* into *i*, as: *durmo durma, durmamos*.

---

26. Ouvir, to hear.

This Verb changes *uvi* into *uç* in all persons in which *mentir* changes *e* into *i*, as: *eu ouço*, I hear — *que eu ouça*, that I may hear.

Imperative Mood.

ouve tu, hear
ouça elle, let him hear

ouçamos nós, let us hear
ouvi vós, hear ye
oução elles, let them hear.

Some writers change *u* into *i*, as: *oiço, oiça*.

Examples.

Quem mente manifesta[1] medo da verdade, e torna-se[2] desprezivel[3] a todo homem de bem[4]. Eu sentia muito sempre que eu ouvia a gente fallar mal d'aquelles de quem tinha aceitado[5] obsequios[6] desinteresseiros[7]. Dormirão muito os seus hospedes: chegárão muito fatigados[8] da longa[9] viagem. O Senhor nos advertirá logo que tiverem vindo os empresarios[10] da construcção[11] da estrada[12] de ferro. Os meninos que mentirem não podem deixar de ser castigados. O Senhor divertio-se n'aquella sociedade? Durma socegado:[13] ninguem lhe ha de fazer mal[14]. E' preciso que não firamos os brios[15] d'esse homem, que são muito bem fundados[16]. Quereriamos que seu filho não mentisse tão desembaraçadamente[17]. Reflicta bem, amigo; parece-me que lhe estão armando um laço[18].

1 to manifest. 2 to become. 3 despicable. 4 honorable men. 5 accept. 6 kindness. 7 disinterested. 8 fatigued. 9 long. 10 the enterpriser. 11 construction. 12 street. 13 quietly. 14 the ill, harm. 15 consciousness. 16 *fundar,* to found. 17 without restraint. 18 to lay a snare.

Se não dormiramos tanto, podiamos todas as manhans gozar[19] d'este bello aspecto[20]. Deve desejar que repitão[21] o exercicio[22] até que souberem bem todos os vocabulos[23]. E' preciso que se vista sem demora[24]. Sigamos o seu conselho.

19 enjoy. 20 aspect. 21 to repeat. 22 the exercise. 23 words. 24 preference.

Exercises.

I often hear people say wicked things. He wants me absolutely[1] not to sleep any more, and yet I am still so tired. Do not lie. If they do not lie, we may calculated on their assistance[2]. I have never slept so well as last night. Have you not dressed yourself yet? Hear what I have to tell you. Let him hear it or not. He sleeps longer than anyone.

1 absolutamente. 2 o auxilio.

---

27. Pór, to place, to put.

Indicative Mood.

Present.

eu ponho, I place	*nós pómos,* we place
tu pões, thou placest	*vós pondes,* you place
elle poem, he places	*elles poem,* they place.

Imperfect.

eu punha, I placed	*nós punhamos,* we placed
tu punhas, thou placedst	*vós punheis,* you placed
elle punha, he placed	*elles punhão,* they placed.

Perfect.

eu puz, I have placed	*nós puzemos,* we have placed
tu puzeste, thou hast placed	*vós puzestes,* you have placed
elle póz, he has placed	*elles puzerão,* they have placed.

Pluperfect.

eu puzera, I had placed
tu puzeras, thou hadst placed
elle puzera, he had placed

nós puzeramos, we had placed
vós puzereis, you had placed
elles puzerão, they had placed.

Future.

eu porei, I shall place
tu porás, thou shalt place
elle porá, he shall place

nós poremos, we shall place
vós poreis, you shall place
elles porão, they shall place.

Conditional.

eu poria, I should place
tu porias, thou shouldst place
elle poria, he should place

nós poriamos, we should place
vós porieis, you should place
elles porião, they should place.

Subjunctive Mood.

Present.

que eu ponha, that I may place
tu ponhas, that thou mayest place
elle ponha, that he may place

que nós ponhamos, that we may place
vós ponhais, that you may place
elles ponhão, that they may place.

Imperfect.

que eu puzera, that I might place
tu puzeras, that thou mightest place
elle puzera, that he might place

que nós puzeramos, that we might place
vós puzereis, that you might place
elles puzerão, that they might place.

Perfect.

que eu puzesse, that I may have placed
tu puzesses, that thou mayest have placed
elle puzesse, that he may have placed

que nós puzessemos, that we may have placed
vós puzesseis, that you may have placed
elles puzessem, that they may have placed.

Future.

quando eu puzer, when I shall place

tu puzeres, when thou shalt place

elle puzer, when he shall place

quando nós puzermos, when we shall place

vós puzerdes, when you shall place

elles puzerem, when they shall place.

Imperative Mood.

põe tu, place thou

ponha elle, let him place

ponhamos nós, let us place

ponde vós, place ye

ponhão elles, let them place.

Gerund: *pondo*, placing.

Participle: *posto*, *posta*, placed.

The Verbs composed by *pór* are conjugated in the same manner, as:

antepór,	to prefer	*oppór*,	to oppose
compór,	to compose	*propór*,	to propose
depór,	to depose	*suppór*,	to suppose
dispór,	to dispose	*presuppór*,	to presuppose.
expór,	to expose		

16.

The following Verbs have two Participles, a regular and an irregular one.

FIRST CONJUGATION.

aceitar,	to accept,	*aceitado*,	*aceito*
enxugar,	to dry,	*enxugado*,	*enxuto*
exceptuar,	to except,	*exceptuado*,	*excepto*
expressar,	to express,	*expressado*,	*expresso*
expulsar,	to expell,	*expulsado*,	*expulso*
gastar,	to spend,	*gastado*,	*gasto*
imprensar,	to print,	*imprensado*,	*impresso*

izentar,	to except,	*izentado,*	*izento*
manifestar,	to manifest,	*manifestado,*	*manifesto*
pagar,	to pay,	*pagado,*	*pago*
salvar,	to save,	*salvado,*	*salvo*
professar,	to act, profess,	*professado,*	*professo*
soltar,	to set at liberty,	*soltado,*	*solto*
sujeitar,	to subject,	*sujeitado,*	*sujeito.*

SECOND CONJUGATION.

absolver,	to acquit,	*absolvido,*	{ *absoluto* / *absolto* }
absorver,	to swallow,	*absorvido,*	*absorto*
accender,	to light,	*accendido,*	*acceso*
corromper,	to corrupt,	*corrompido,*	*corrupto*
eleger,	to elect,	*elegido,*	*eleito*
encher,	to fill,	*enchido,*	*cheio*
envolver,	to envelope,	*envolvido,*	*envolto*
escrever,	to write,	*escrevido,*	*escrito*
incorrer,	to incur (a penalty),	*incorrido,*	*incurso*
interromper,	to interrupt,	*interrompido,*	*interrupto*
morrer,	to die,	*morrido,*	*morto*
prender,	to take (into charge),	*prendido,*	*preso*
romper,	to break (open),	*rompido,*	*roto*
suspender,	to postpone,	*suspendido,*	*suspenso*
torcer,	to turn,	*torcido,*	*torto.*

THIRD CONJUGATION.

abrir,	to open,	*abrido,*	*aberto*
affligir,	to afflict,	*affligido,*	*afflicto*
concluir,	to close, shut,	*concluido,*	*concluso*
contrahir,	to contract,	*contrahido,*	*contracto*
cubrir,	to cover,	*cubrido,*	*cuberto*
distinguir,	to distinguish,	*distinguido,*	*distincto*
distrahir,	to abstract,	*distrahido,*	*distracto*
erigir,	to erect,	*erigido,*	*erecto*
exhaurir,	to exhaust,	*exhaurido,*	*exhausto*
expellir,	to expell,	*expellido,*	*expulso*
exprimir,	to express,	*exprimido,*	*expresso*

exstinguir,	to extinguish,	*extinguido,*	*extincto*
extrahir,	to extract,	*extrahido,*	*extracto*
frigir,	to fry,	*frigido,*	*frito*
imprimir,	to impress,	*imprimido,*	*impresso*
incluir,	to shut up,	*incluido,*	*incluso*
inserir,	to insert,	*inserido,*	*inserto*
opprimir,	to oppress,	*opprimido,*	*oppresso*
possuir,	to possess,	*possuido,*	*possesso*
reprimir,	to repress,	*reprimido,*	*represso*
submergir,	to submerge,	*submergido,*	*submerso*
supprimir,	to suppress,	*supprimido,*	*suppresso*
surgir,	to anchor,	*surgido,*	*surto.*

The first or regular form of these Participles is generally used for the compound tenses, whilst the second or irregular form is generally used with *ser* or *estar*.

17.

Impersonal Verbs

are only used in the third person Singular, they are:

Chover, to rain	— *chove,* it rains
relampager / *fuzilar* } to lighten	— *relampaga* / *fuzila* } it lightens
trovejar, to thunder	— *troveja,* it thunders
choviscar, to drizzle (rain)	— *chovisca,* it drizzles
nevar, to snow	— *neva,* it snows
gelar, to freeze	— *gela,* it freezes.

They follow those Conjugations to which they belong.

Adverbs.

18.

1. Adverbs of Time.

Hoje, to-day
agora, now
hontem, yesterday
presentemente, at present
antehontem, the day before
    yesterday
antigamente, in times past
ultimamente, lastly
recentemente, lately

amanhãa, to-morrow
logo, directly
depois de amanhãa, the day
    after to-morrow
daqui por diante, from hence,
    in future
sempre, always
desde, since
ainda, yet.

2. Adverbs of Place.

aqui, here
ali, *acolá*, there
arriba, above
abaixo, below
além, on the other side

daquem, on this side
á mão direita, to the right
á mão esquerda, to the left
d'ali. from here.

3. Adverbs of Number and Comparison.

primeiramente, firstly
segundamente, secondly
em terceiro lugar, thirdly
depois, afterwards
raramente, *de maravilha*, rarely
mais, more
menos, less
tão
como-se } almost

como, as
assim, just so, the same
melhor, better
peior, worse
quasi, almost
em parte, partly
quando muito, highest
quando menos, least.

4. Adverbs of Manner and Kind.

muito, very
bem, good, well
mal, bad
pouco, little
assaz, enough
demasiadamente, too much
sufficientemente, sufficient

abundantemente, abundantly
mesmo, even
apenas, scarcely
senão, only
principalmente, chiefly
em geral, generally, altogether.

---

5. Adverbs of Affirmation and Negation.

sim, yes
certamente, certainly
verdadeiramente, indeed
não, no
nada, nothing
talvez
pode ser } perhaps
quiça

quando? when?
como? how?
porque? why?
quanto? how much?
onde? where?
aonde? whereto?

The Adverbs are not declined, but some are compared like the Adjectives, as:

mais ricamente,   richer
menos ricamente,   less rich
tão ricamente,   just as rich
muito ricamente,   very rich
o mais ricamente,   the richest;

Superl.
bem, good, formes the Com.: *melhor* — *optimamente*
mal, bad,   -   -   -   *peior* — *pessimamente*.

19.

The following Adverbs are principally in use:

agora, now	*de improviso* / *improvisamente*, extempore
hoje, to-day	
amanhãa, to-morrow	*quasi, casi*, almost
amanhãa pela manhãa, to-morrow-morning	*então*, then
	desde então, since
depois de amanhãa, the day after to-morrow	*desde quando?* since when?
	de quando ha? how long ago?
frequentamente, frequently, often	*quando bem* / *ainda quando*, even
nunca, never	*quando muito*, highest, at latest
ordinariamente, generally	*quando menos*, at least
jamais, never	*cá*, here
tarde, late	*alli*, there
cedo, early	*ahi*, there, where (you are)
daqui por diante, in future	*acóla*, there
ultimamente, lastly, at latest	*traz* / *detraz*, behind
recentemente, lately	
logo, soon	*para traz*, backwards
depois, afterwards	*isto he*, that is to say
abundantemente, abundantly	*em vez, em lugar*, instead
com razão, justamente, in justice	*tambem*, also
absolutamente, absolutely	*tanto que* / *logo que*, as soon as
já para já, immediately	
com condição, under the condition	*acaso*, accidentally
	ainda, yet
actualmente, actually, at present	*finalmente*, at last
de proposito, purposely	*muito*, much, very
admiravelmente / *maravilhosamente*, admirable	*depressa*, quickly
	aqui, here
as mil maravilhas, exquisitely	*até*, until
astutamente, artfully	*bem*, well, good
atraiçoadamente, traitorously	*mal*, bad
de maravilha, very rarely	*como*, how, as
a miudo, often	*como?* how?
assim / *tão*, so, equally so	*primeiro que*, before that
	primeiro que tudo, before all
apressa, quickly, in haste	*fora*, out, out of
facilmente, easily	*já*, already
ao avesso, reversedly	*abaixo*, below
as avessas, reversedly	*acima*, above

lde, in vain
  for, before
nente, together
amente, entirely
dor, round about
nente, foolishly
damente, boldly
ente, happily
nhosamente, infamously
se quer, even if
  more
, less
yes
no

onde, where
nada, nothing
de cór, by heart
em vão, in vain
escassamente, scarcely, rarely
em fin, at last
longe, long, far
verdadeiramente, truly
dentro, therein
as vezes, sometimes
de vagar, slowly
quando, when
quanto, how much.

Prepositions.

20.

The Prepositions most in use are the following:

om
n
, in, within
  on, over
o} under
e, before
} behind
  between
after
 by, near, at
 of, from
fter

antes, before
depois, after
durante, during
desde, since
com, with
excepto, except
fora} besides
além}
sem, without
contra, against
a pezar, notwithstanding
não obsante, in spite of
para com, against
acerca, in respect
por, through
mediante, by means of.

21.

The following are used with the Genitive:

além dos mares,	on the other side of the seas
além d'isso,	besides this one
acerca daquelle negocio,	as to that business
aquem or *daquem dos mares,*	on this side of the seas
antes do dia,	before daybreak
diante de Deos,	before God
dentro da igreja,	within the church
de traz do palacio,	behind the palace
debaixo da mesa,	under the table
em cima da mesa,	upon the table
ao redor or *em contorno da cidade,*	round about the town
perto de Londres,	near London
fora da casa,	out of the house
fora de perigo,	out of danger
depois da cea,	after the supper
defronte de minha casa,	opposite to my house
defronte da igreja,	opposite the church;

Dative:

quanto áquillo,	with regard to that
pegado á muralha,	at, near the wall
desde o bico do pé até á cabeza,	from head to foot;

Accusative:

perante o juiz,	before the judge
durante o inverno,	during the winter
traz do templo,	behind the temple
entre os homens,	among men
sobre a mesa,	on the table
conforme á lei,	according to the law
segundo á ordem,	in consequence of the order
por amor de Deos.	for God's sake
pelo mundo,	through the world
pela rua,	through the street
contra elles,	against them.

A (to), *eu vou a Londres,* I go to London,
   voltar a Portugal, to return to Portugal,
   não tem nada que fazer }
   não tem nada a fazer } he has nothing to do.

De (from), *vir de França,* I come from France,
   vir das Indias, I come from India,
   sahir de Londres, I go from London
            (to leave London),
      de noite, by night,
      de dia, by day.

Por (by, from), *por mar e por terra,* by sea and by land.

Conjunctions.

22.

E, and
tambem }
outrosim } also
tambem — como, as well — as
não sómente — mas tambem,
   not only — but also
ora — ora, soon — soon
em primeiro lugar, firstly
então, then
além disso }
de mais } further
depois, afterwards
em fim, at last
em parte — em parte, partly
   — partly
ou — ou, either — or

nem — nem, neither — nor
tão, so
assim, thus
porém }
mas } but
com tudo, notwithstanding
ainda que, although
assim, therefore
porque, because
pois, there
afim, that
se não, else
com tanto que, taking for granted
   that
bem que, certainly, indeed.

23.

que, that
nomeadamente, namely
se, whether

comó, as
a saber, viz
excepto, alem, except

onde, where	*por isso,* why
donde, whence	*porque,* because
quando, when	*por, pois,* there
desde que, since	*afim que* \ that
durante que, whilst, during	*para que* / that
antes, before	*se,* if
depois que \ afterwards	*se, posto que,* in case
depois de / afterwards	*se não que,* if not
como, as	*com tanto que,* in case
como tambem, as soon as	*ainda que,* although
tão — como, so — as	*não obstante,* notwithstanding
assim — que, so that	*tanto — tanto,* the — the.

Examples.

Francezes e Inglezes,	Frenchmen and Englishmen.
Nem este, nem aquelle.	Neither these, nor those.
Ou este, ou aquelle.	Either this one, or that one.
Nem mais, nem menos.	Neither more, nor less.
Quer o faça, quer não tudo para mim he o mesmo.	It is indifferent to me whether he does it or not.
Quer seja verdade, quer não.	Whether it be true or not.
Antes quero pedir que furtar.	I will rather beg than steal.
Antes morrerei que dizer-volo.	I will rather die than tell it to you.

Interjections

may be divided according to the various passions or emotions expressed by them.

Of Joy: *Ah! ho!*
Of Pain: *Ai! apre!*
Of Fear: *Ai Jesus! eh, eh! ai de mim!*
Of Abhorrence: *Va-se embora! passa fora!*
Of Surprise: *Oh! Ah!*
Urging or Exhorting: *Ora vamos! animo, animo! arreda! hola! sentido!*
Silencing: *Chiton! calla a boca! calai-vos!*
Wishing: *O provera a Deos!*

Reading Lessons.

1.

Em um ajuntamento [1] de senhoras e homens suscitou-se[2] a questão [3] de qual era o paiz [4] melhor [5] para se habitar [6]; e dizendo uma que Londres, outra que Pariz, este que o Brazil, aquelle que a Austria ou a Italia, disse uma senhora mui presumida [7]: „Pois [8] eu dou [9] a primazia [10] ao celibato, pois tenho ouvido dizer á meu irmão padre [11], que he de todos os estados o mais perfeito."

1 meeting. 2 to ask. 3 the question. 4 land. 5 better. 6 to live. 7 presumptuous. 8 as. 9 I give. 10 the preference. 11 the priest.

2.

Certo [1] juiz de fóra [2] tendo queixas do povo [3] que os arrematantes da vacca [4] só matavão [5] um boi [6] cada dia d'assouge [7], e que este não chegava [8] para todos, e ao mesmo tempo [9] ouvindo dizer aos ditos arrematantes que dous bois erão de sobejo [10]; mandou [11] por seu respeitando despacho que cada dia d'assougue se matasse boi e meio.

1 a certain. 2 judge who has studied. 3 the people. 4 the priviledged butchers of beef. 5 *matar*, to kill, to slaughter. 6 the ox. 7 *açougue*, the slaughter-house. 8 *chegar*, to suffice. 9 at the same time. 10 too much. 11 to order.

3.

Dizia o P. Antonio Vieira, que toda a fortuna d'um homem de corte [1] consistia em saber adular [2], mentir [3], furtar [4], e repartir [5].

1 courtier. 2 to flatter. 3 to lie. 4 to steal. 5 to divide.

4.

Na desgraçada [1] morte [2] do Principe D. Affonso, disse El-Rei Dom João II. seu pai: „No excessivo sentimento em que vivo da morte de meu filho, só me consola parecer-me que Deos se lembrou [3] d'este reino [4]; porque o Principe não era para Rei dos Portuguezes: os Portuguezes hão de mister Rei de bronze. Era o Principe inclinado a delicias [5].

1 unfortunate. 2 death. 3 *lembrar-se*, to remember. 4 kingdom. 5 pleasure.

5.

Levantando [1] El-Rei D. João I. o sitio [2], que tinha posto a Coria, disse: „Grande falta [3] nos fizerão os cavalheiros da taboa redonda [4]; porque se elles aqui estivérão, não nos levantáramos desta cidade sem a render [5]. Respondeo Mem Rodrigues de Vasconcellos: „Não faltarão por certo, senhor, aqui esses cavalheiros; porque aqui está Martim Vasques da Cunha, que he tão bom, como dizem o foi D. Galaz; Gonçalo Vasques Coutinho, que he tão bom como D. Tristão; João Fernandes Pacheco, que não deve nada a Lancarote; e aqui estou eu, que não mereço [6] menos [7] que qualquer d'elles: O certo he, senhor, que só faltou aqui o bom Rei Artur, que os sabía estimar, e animar com mercês grandes.

1 to raise. 2 the siege. 3 want. 4 round table. 5 surrender. 6 to be worth. 7 less.

6.

Quando El-Rei D. Sebastião quiz[1] fazer[2] a jornada de África, determinou avistar-se em N. Senhora de Guadalupe com El-Rei Philippe seu tio[3]; para se ajustar[4] esta funcção[5] veio[6] de Castella o duque[7] d'Alva, cavalheiro mui soberbo[8], e pouco affeiçoado aos Portuguezes, e de cá foi o conde[9] de Redondo. Entre a pratica[10] que tiverão, lhe perguntou[11] o duque que fidalgos vinhão com El-Rei Dom Sebastião; porque com El-Rei vinha elle, e outros como elle. Respondeo-lhe o conde: „Com El-Rei meu senhor vem o duque de Bragança, o de Aveiro, e o marquez[12] de Villa-Real; e fidalgos razos[13], como eu e vós, vem muitos."

1 *querer*, to wish. 2 to make. 3 uncle. 4 to arrange. 5 business. 6 he came (*vir*). 7 duke. 8 proud. 9 the count. 10 the discussion. 11 to ask. 12 marquis. 13 the low gentry.

7.

Pedindo[1] um pobre[2] esmola[3] a Philippe II. lhe dizia que se lembrasse erão irmãos: e perguntando-lhe El-Rei por que quarte, respondèo por Adão. Mandou[4]-lhe El-Rei dar um real. Replicou[5] o pobre que aquella esmola não era d'um irmão Rei. „Sé a todos os meus irmãos", disse Philippe, „eu désse outro tanto[6], já não teria[7] real que dar."

1 *pedir*, to beg. 2 poor. 3 alms. 4 ordered. 5 reply. 6 just as much. 7 I would have.

8.

Christovão Colon foi o primeiro que com audaz[1] fortaleza[2] navegou o oceano, o descobrio[3] as Indias de Castella; pelo que mereceo que os Reis Catholicos o fizessem duque de Beraguas. Estava uma noite[4] ceando[5] com outros cavalheiros seus amigos; e dizendo-lhe um que aquella façanha a poderia obrar qualquer outro, se lhe dessem o socorro[6], que fosse necessario, dissimulou Christovão Colon, e tirando um

1 audacious. 2 fortitude. 3 discovered. 4 night. 5 *cear*, to sup 6 assistance.

ovo do prato, perguntou aos demais fidalgos· se poderia algum fazer que aquelle ovo estivesse levantado[8], sem que se arrimasse[9] a cousa alguma? Respondêrão todos, que não podia ser[10]. Pegou[11] no ovo Christovão Colon, e dando com elle mansamente[12] na mesa[13], lhe fez uma pequena[14] móssa[15], e o poz muito direíto. Rírão-se[16] todos, e dísse Colon: „Nenhum[17] de Vossas Mercês[18] ha que não acha facil navegar o oceano, depois que eu de lá vím; porém he certo, que se eu não fôra o primeiro, nenhum seria o segundo.“

7 egg. 8 to stand erect. 9 to assist. 10 that it could not be. 11 *pegar,* to take up. 12 quiet. 13 table. 14 small. 15 break. 16 *rir-se,* to laugh. 17 nobody. 18 of your honours.

9.

Um Mahometano consultando a Aischeh mulher de Mahometo, lhe pedio uma regra[1] para bem víver; e ella lhe respondeo: „Reconhece[2] um só Deos, refrêa[3] a tua lingua, reprime[4] as tuas paixões[5], adquire sciencia, vive constante na tua religião, abstem-te de fazer mal[6], frequenta os bons, encobre[7] os defeitos do teu proximo[8], soccorre[9] os pobres, e espera a eternidade por recompensa.

1 rule. 2 recognise. 3 restrict. 4 suppress. 5 passions. 6 to do evil. 7 cover. 8 neighbour. 9 assist.

10.

Querendo certo homem desquitar-se[1] de sua mulher, com quem tinha pouca paz[2], appareceo[3] para este fim[4] diante[5] do Provisor. Estranhou[6] elle a proposta[7], porque conhecia a mulher, e era de boas qualidades: „Porque quereis deixar[8] vossa mulher?“ (lhe perguntou o Provisor): „Não he virtuosa?“ — „Sim, senhor“; respondeo o homem. — „Não he rica?“ — „Sim, senhor.“ Emfim[9] a todas as cousas, sobre que era perguntado, respondia em abono seu. Com que lhe

1 to divorce. 2 peace. 3 appeared. 4 for this purpose. 5 before. 6 to surprise. 7 the proposition. 8 to leave. 9 in fine.

dísse o Provisor: „Pois se vossa mulher tem tantas cousas boas, porque quereis desquitar-vos della?" A isto o homem, descalçando [10] um sapato [11], perguntou ao Provisor: „Senhor, este sapato não he novo?" — „Sim", respondeo o Provisor. Accrescentou [12]: „não está bem feito [13]?" — „Sim, ao que parece", respondeo o Provisor. — „Não he de bom cordavão, e de boa sola?" — Respondeo do mesmo modo que sim. „Pois vê Vossa Mercê com tudo isso [14] (disse o descontente marido [15]), pois eu quero tirar este sapato, e calçar outro, porque eu sei muito bem aonde [16] me aperta [17], e faz mancar [18], e Vossa Mercê não o sabe.

10 to take off. 11 the shoe. 12 to add. 13 *fazer*, to make. 14 with all that. 15 husband. 16 where. 17 pinch. 18 to make tame.

11.

Botocudos.

Estes Indios dominão [1] na cordilheira [2] habitada [3] por seus maiores [4] os Aimorés, de cuja [5] barbaridade ainda guardão sementes. Quando os Portuguezes começárão [6] a povoar [7] o Brazil tiverão de guerrear com os ferozes [8] Aimorés, a quem dizem [9] que derão [10] o nome de Botocudos, de boto, e codea [11], por isso que os Indios desta nação [12] erão rolhos, e trazião [13] o corpo [14] coberto d'uma codea de gomma [15] copal com que se pintavão [16] para se preservarem das ferretoadas [17] dos mosquitos e outros insectos. Os Botocudos são mais brancos [18] que a maior parte dos demais [19] Indios do Brazil, porém, como seus ascendentes os Aimorés, costumão [20] pintar a cara [21] e mais partes do corpo. Dividem-se em varias tribus ou cabildas [22], cada [23] uma com seu cabo [24], que tem um poder [25] absoluto sobre os seus [26] em os negocios de maior importancia como são o caça [27], a guerra [28] e a escolha [29] de uma nova morada [30]; mas na aldea [31] limita-se toda a sua

1 govern. 2 mountain chain. 3 inhabited. 4 ancestors. 5 whose. 6 to begin. 7 to populate. 8 wild. 9 *dizer*, to say. 10 they gave (*dar*). 11 the rind. 12 nation. 13 to carry. 14 the body. 15 gum. 16 *pintar*, to paint. 17 sting. 18 white. 19 the others. 20 to have the practice. 21 face. 22 hordes. 23 each. 24 leader. 25 power. 26 over his tribe. 27 the chase. 28 war. 29 the choice. 30 place of residence. 31 village.

autoridade a compôr as desavenças que são entre elles mui frequentes. Este lugar não he hereditario, escolhe-se para elle o mais bravo, e por vezes[32] o mais atrevido[33] se proclama por chefe da tribu, sobre tudo se por ventura o que os commandava vem a morrer. Os Botocudos tem as espadoas[34] largas, o pescoço[35] curto, o nariz[36] chato, as macãas[37] do rosto proeminentes, os pés[38] pequenos, as extremidades inferiores delgadas[39], mas nervosas. Furão orelhas[40], e o beiço inferior[41], e enfião no buraco[42] uma rodella de páo[43]. São vingativos[44] e traidores[45], posto que tinhão um exterior alegre e um ar[46] de franqueza. Não tem especie alguma de culto; considerão[47] o sol[48] como uma divindade a que chamão[49], e reverenceão ainda mais a lua[50], quando com sua luz os protege em suas excursões nocturnas. Amão e imitão as ceremonias religiosas dos christãos, quanto isto póde compadecer-se com a vida nomada que fazem, assim que são de todos os Indios os que mais custão a civilzar-se.

32 sometimes. 33 bold. 34 shoulder. 35 neck. 36 nose. 37 cheeks. 38 foot. 39 thin. 40 ears. 41 the underlip. 42 a hole. 43 wooden. 44 vindictive. 45 traitorous. 46 an air. 47 to look upon. 48 the sun. 49 to call. 50 the moon.

12.

As grutas[1] do inferno[2].

Deo-se[3] este nome ás cavernas naturaes que se achão[4] na montanha em que estão assentadas a povoação e fortaleza[5] da Nova-Coimbra, na provincia de Mato-Grosso e sobre a margem direita[6] do Paraguai. No vertente[7] septentrional[8] da montanha existe uma abertura que dá passo[9] a duas especies de antecamaras, 1 de braca[10] e meia de comprido[11], e 1 de largo[12], e outra algum tanto maior. Desce-se para ellas por uma ladeira que tem obra de 20 braças de comprimento[13], guarnecida de estalactitas, que provêm da filtração continua da abobada. No cabo[14] da ladeira entra-se n'uma salla parecida com uma mesquita[15], de cuja abobada pendem estalac-

1 grotto. 2 hell. 3 one has given. 4 to find, *achar-se*. 5 the fortress. 6 on the right shore. 7 slope. 8 northern. 9 which form the entrance. 10 fathom. 11 long. 12 wide. 13 length. 14 at the end. 15 Mosque.

titas de differentes fórmas e tamanhos [16], e o mesmo se observa no chão. A' esquerda [17] a parede se acha revestida d'uma oicrustação d'espalto, que com o reflexo da luz arremeda uma snberba cascata. Póde esta salla ter 50 braças de comprido e 18 de largo, e no fundo della existe um espaço de 6 braças pelo menos coberto d'agua limpida porém de máo sabor [18], que dá da parte de fóra [19] origem a um ribeiro [20] represado frequentemente pelas aguas do Paraguai, nas cheias [21] que alagão todos os annos por varias vezes os campos vizinhos. Os naturaes [22] do paiz não se atrevião [23] a entrar n'estas grutas que forão pela primeira vez exploradas pelo engenheiro [24] Ricardo Franco d'Almeida Serra, em 1791, levando em sua companbia o naturalista Alexandre Rodriguez Ferreira que as debuxou [25] e descreveo [26]. Em 1795, varias pessoas [27] curiosas entrárão n'ellas e com fachas virão que no ribeiro que as aguas ali formavão havião jacarés [28], e que um d'elles tinha uma pata de menos.

16 size. 17 on the left. 18 bad taste. 19 from the outside. 20 rivulet. 21 inundation. 22 inhabitants. 23 attempt. 24 engineer. 25 to draw. 26 to describe. 27 persons. 28 crocodile.

Vida de Luiz de Camoens.

Este famosissimo Poeta portuguez nasceo em Lisboa pelos annos de 1524. Forão seus pais Simão Vaz de Camoens e Anna de Sá Macedo, ambos de nobres e antigas familias de Portugal.

Applicou-se ao estudo das Humanidades, em que sahio insigne. Deo-se singularmente á Poesia, e forão tam felizes seus ensaios, que por elles começou, sendo ainda muito moço, ser conhecido e estimado na Corte.

Passou algums annos sem outro emprego mais, que os galanteios e diversoens, em que costumão gastar o tempo os de sua idade e qualidade; em lhe que se rendeo mui deveras á formosura de certa mulher, em que acharão benigno e honesto agrado os seus rendimentos.

Mas os parentes levarão tánto á mal a pretensão de Luiz Camoens, que o fizerão com varios pretextos sahir desterrado de Lisboa. Este foi o primeiro golpe com que a fortuna para elle sempre adversa, o começou a ferir.

Foi á Ceuta, onde nos exercicios das armas mostrou, que não era menos valeroso que entendido. Em hum encontro com os Mouros perdeo hum olho, e nesta infelicidade teve a grande consolação de não poder ver, sem ser visto com huma nobre testemunha de seu valor.

Encommendou-lhe depois certo Fidalgo, que matasse a hum seu adversario, o qual, como Camoens, tambem era torto de hum olho. Aceitou a commissão com facilidade e desafogo de soldado; mas esqueceo della com temor de bom Christão. Culpando lhe o Fidalgo o omissão, respondeó gracejando:

> Logo lhe não vi bom geito
> Quando vo-lo dei por morto;
> Porque torto matar torto,
> Não me pareceo direito.

Cessada a causa do seu desterro, voltou para Lisboa, onde achou seus pais cahidos em pobreza; motivo, que se resolveo a navegar para a India, desenganado de tornar mais a Portugal.

Adquirio naquellas partes illustre nome nos casos militares daquelle tempo; mas os premios forão muito desiguaes aos seus merecimentos. Apenas lhe derão certo officio, que foi servir em Macao cidade que os Portuguezes começavão a fundar na China. Della sahio com algums cabedaes e voltando á Goa, os perdeo em hum horrendo naufragio, do que escapou á nado não salvando que sua pessoa e sua Lusiada, que ja então havia composto em grande parte.

Passou de Goa a Lisboa, seguido e perseguido sempre de infortunios e perigos no mar e na terra, e de más correspondencias de falsos amigos. Dedicou a sua Lusiada á **El Rei Dom** Sebastião, que lhe deo huma limitada tença, que por ser de tam pouco porte, e por encontrar na cobrança mais difficuldades, do que os ceitis de que ella constava; veio a cahir em pobreza tam extrema, que chegou a viver de esmolas, que de noite pedia pelas ruas de Lisboa hum rapaz chamado Antonío, que trouxéra da India.

Em huma occasião lhe fallou o Duque de Aveiro, e sabendo delle, que não tinha de jantar naquelle dia, lhe *perguntou que* cousa queria lhe mandasse da sua mesa? Respondendo Camoens, que lhe bastava huma gallinha, lha prometeo o Duque; mas não lhe lembrou a promessa se não muito depois de ter jantado; não havendo ja gallinha, mandou hum prato de vaca a Luiz Camoens, qual pelo mesmo criado do Duque lhe mandou logo a resposta seguinte:

> Ja eu vi á taverneiro
> Vender vaca por carneiro;
> Mas não vi por vida minha
> Vender vaca por gallinha,
> Se não o Duque de Aveiro.

Não se pode assaz lastimar hum tamanho desamparo em homem tam insigne, e que foi huma das primeiras glorias da nacão portugueza. Não accuse-se ao Rei, que era menino; mas quem não condemnará aos Ministros e Grandes, que então vivião, aos quaes pudéra aquelle portentoso engenho dar vida immortal, se elles o ajudassem a manter a sua com huma limitada porção. Mas he justo castigo da miseria ou ignorancia dos taes, acabar-se por sua morte a sua memoria, eternisando-se ao mesmo tempo a dos Varoens sabios e valerosos, por mais que fossem desestimados na vida.

O extremo desemparo, em que Luiz Camoens se chegou a ver, lhe causou huma tam profunda tristeza, que bastou a lhe accelerar a morte. Ja nos ultimos annos vivia tam alheo de si mesmo e tam entregne ás consideraçoens da sua desgraça que parecia outro muito mais differente, do que havia sido.

Pedio lhe por aquelle tempo certo Cavalleiro illustre, que lhe quizesse traduzir em verso portuguez os sete Psalmos Penitenciaes, facilitando-o a promptidão com que fazia os versos; ao que elle respondeo: Quando eu os fazia, achava-me em idade florente favorecido das damas e estimado dos amigos, e não me faltava o necessario. Agora tudo isto me falta, e ahi está o meu Antonio, que me pede duas moedas de cobre para carvão, e não as tenho para lhas dar.

Entre innumeraveis miserias morreo finalmente no anno 1569; algums dizem em hum hospital, unico refugio dos desamparados.

Foi sepultado na igreja do mosteiro de S. Anna, logo a entrada da parte esquerda, sem algum sinal que distinguisse a sua sepultura; até que no anno de 1595 Dom Gonçalo Coutinho, Cavalleiro illustre, lhe levantou hum nobre tumulo com a inscripção seguinte:

Aqui jaz LUIZ de CAMOENS, Principe
Dos Poetas de seu tempo;
Viveo pobre e miseravelmente e assim morreo
Anno de MDLXIX.

Foi de Camoens nobilissimo em sangue, brioso soldado, discreto cortezão, alegre e prompto nos ditos, facil no trato, constante nas amizades, de natural liberal e generoso, firme amante da patria por mais que ella lhe pagava com ingratidoens, grande avaliador de acçoens heroicas, amartellado da verdade, e nimigo jurado da lisonja.

A sua Lusiada contem a proba concludente da facilidade, da propriedade, da copia, da elegancia e da doçura, graça e energia da lingua portugueza, que talvez os seus mesmos Naturaes desprezão.

Não faltou, quem lhe quiz arguir nas suas obras algums defeitos contra as leis da Poesia; mas são veniaes. Ainda que murmura a emulação de poucos e nescios; tem Camoens de sua parte o applauso universal das mais sabias naçoens da Europa.

Poesias.

SONETO.

Alma minha gentil, que te partiste
Tam cedo desta vida descontente?
Repousa la no ceo eternamente
E viva eu ca na terra sempre triste!

Se la no assento ethereo, onde subiste,
Memoria desta vida se consente:
Não te esqueças daquelle amor ardente
Que ja nos olhos meus tam puro viste.

E se veres, que pode merecer-te
Alguma cousa a dor, que me ficou
Da magoa sem remedio de perder-te;

Roga a Deos, que teus annos encortou,
Que tam cedo de ca me leve a ver-te,
Quam cedo de meus olhos te levou.

Camoens.

SONETO.

Mudão-se os tempos, mudão-se as vontades,
Muda-se o ser, muda-se a confiança;
Todo o mundo he composto de mudança,
Tomando sempre novas qualidades.

Continuamente vemos novidades
Differentes em tudo da esperança:
Do mal ficão as magoas na lembrança
E do bem, se algum houve, as saúdades.

O tempo cobre o chão de verde manto
Que ja coberta foi de neve fria;
E em mim converte em choro o doce canto.

E afora eate mudar-se cada dia,
Outra mudança faz de mor espanto,
Que não se muda ja como sohia.

Camoens.

Em occasião da morte da Infanta Dona Maria, filha de
El Rei Dom Manoel.

SONETO.

Que levas, cruel morte? Hum claro dia.
A que horas o tomaste? Amanhecendo.
Entendes o que levas? Não entendo.
Pois quem to fez lever? Quem o entendia.

Seu corpo quem o goza? A terra fria.
Como ficou sua luz? Anoitecendo.
Lusitania que diz? Fica dizendo;
Emfim não mereci Dona Maria!

Mataste, quem a via? Ja morto estava.
Que diz o seu amor? Fallar não ousa.
E quem o faz calar? Minha vontade.

Na morte que ficou? Saudade brava.
Que fica la que ver? Nenhuma cousa;
Ma fica que chorar sua beldade.

Camoens.

SONETO.

Horas breves do meu contentamento,
Nunca me pareceo, quando vos tinha,
Que vos visse mudadas tam azinha
Em tam compridos dias de tormento.

Os meus Castellos, que fundei no vento,
O vento mos levou, que mos sostinha.
Do mal, que me ficou, a culpa he minha;
Pois sobre cousas vams fiz fundamento.

Amor com falsas mostras apparece;
Tudo possivel faz, tudo assegura,
E logo no melhor desapparece.

O! damno grande e grande desventura!
Por hum pequeno bem, que desfalece,
Aventurar hum bem, que sempre dura.

Do Infante Dom Luiz, filho de El Rei Dom Manoel.

DECIMA.

Os boms vi sempre passar
No mundo graves tormentos,
E para mais m' espantar
Os males vi sempre nadar
Em mares de contentamento.

Cuidando alcançar assim
O bem tam mal ordenado,
Fui mau, mas fui castigado;
Assim que só para mim
Anda o mundo concertado.

Comoens.

DA LUSIADA.

I.

As armas e os varões assinalados,
Que da occidental praia Lusitana
Por mares nunca d' antes navegados
Passarão ainda alem da Taprobana;
Em perigos e guerras esforçados,
Mais do que promettia a força humana,
Entre gente remota edificarão
Novo reino, que tanto sublimarão.

II.

E tambem as memorias gloriosas
Daquelles Reis, que forão dilatando
A fé, o imperio; e as terras viciosas
De Africa e de Asia andarão devastando;
E aquelles que por obras valerosas
Se vão da lei da morte libertando;
Cantando espalharei por toda parte,
Se á tanto me ajudar o engenho, e arte.

III.

Cessem do sabio Grego, e do Troiano
As navegações grandes, que fizerão;
Cale-se de Alexandre e de Trajano
A fama das victorias, que tiverão:
Que eu canto o peito illustre Lusitano,
A quem Neptuno, e Marte obedecerão;
Cesse tudo o que a Musa antiga canta
Que outro valor mais alto se alevanta!

IV.

E vos, Tagides minhas! pois creado
Tendes em min um novo engenho ardente;
Se sempre em verso humilde celebrado
Foi di mi vosso rio alegremente:
Dai-me agora um som alto e sublimado,
Um estilo grandiloquo e corrente,
Porque de vossas aguas Phebo ordene
Que não tenhão inveja ás de Hippocrene.

V.

Dai-me uma furia grande e sonorosa,
E não de agreste avena, ou frauta ruda;
Mas de tuba canora e bellicosa,
Que o peito acende, e a côr ao gesto muda;
Dai-me igual canto aos feitos da famosa
Gente vossa, á que Marte tanto ajuda;
Que se espalhe, e se cante no universo,
Se tam sublime preço cabe em verso.

VI.

E vós, o' bem nascida segurança
Da Lusitana antiga liberdade,
E não menos certissima esperança
De augmento da pequena Christandade:
Vós, ó novo temor da Maura lança,
Maravilha fatal da nossa idade,
Dado ao mundo por Deos, que tôdo o mande,
Para do mundo á Deos dar parte grande.

VII.

Vós, tenro e novo ramo florecente
De uma arvore de Christo mais amada
Que nenhuma nascida no Occidente,
Cesarea, ou Christianissima chamada:
Vede-o no vosso escudo, que presente
Vos amostra a victoria ja passada,
Na qual vos deo por armas, e deixou
As que elle para si na cruz tomou.

VIII.

Vós, poderoso Rei, cujo alto imperio
O sol logo em nascendo vé primeiro;
Vé-o tambem no meio do hemisferio;
E quando desce, o deixa derradeiro:
Vós, que esperamos jugo e vituperio
Do torpe Ismaelita cavalleiro,
Do Turco oriental e de Gentio
Que inda bebe o licor do santo rio:

IX.

Inclinai por um pouco a magestade,
Que n'esse tenro gesto vos contemplo;
Que ja se mostra qual na inteira idade,
Quando subindo ireis ao eterno templo;
Os olhos da real benignidade
Ponde no chão: vereis um novo exemplo
De amor dos patrios feitos valerosos
Em versos divulgado numerosos.

X.

Vereis amor de patria não movido
De premio vil, mas alto e quasi eterno.
Que não he premio vil, ser conhecido
Por um pregão do ninho meu paterno.
Ouvi, vereis o nome engrandecido
Daquelles, de quem sois Senhor superno
E julgareis qual he mais excellente,
Se ser do mundo Rei, se de tal gente.

XI.

Ouvi; que não vereis com vãs façanhas
Fantasticas, fingidas, mentirosas
Louvar os vossos, como nas estranhas
Musas, de engrandecer-se desejosas.
As verdadeiras vossas são tamanhas,
Que excedem as sonhadas fabulosas:
Que excedem Rodamonte e o vão Rugeiro
E Orlando, indaque fora verdadeiro.

XII.

Não deixarão meus versos esquecidos
Aquelles, que nos reinos la d'Aurora
Se fizerão por armas tam subidos
Vossa bandeira sempre vencedora:
Um Pacheco fortissimo; e os temidos
Almeidas, por quem sembre o Tejo chora:
Alboquerque terrivel, Castro forte
E outros em que 'poder não teve a morte.

Models of Letters.

To begin a letter.

Sir,	*Senhor Dom*
Gentlemen,	*Senhores*
Madam,	*Senhora*
„ (to a young Lady)	*Senhorita*
My dear Sir,	*Meu querida senhor*
My dear friend,	*Meu caro amigo.*

To end a letter.

I have the honor to be your Lordship's etc.	*Tenho a honra de ser, illustrissimo senhor.*
Most obedient Servant,	*Muito humilde e muito obediente criado.*
Yours very truly,	*Seu muito affectuoso.*
Always yours,	*Sempre seu.*
Your friend,	*Seu amigo.*
Your affectionate friend.	*Seu affectuoso amigo.*

Modellos de Cartas.

1.

O senhor e a senhora B. fazem os seus comprimentos e civilidades ao senhor e á senhora F. e pedem-lhes que lhes fação a honra de vir jantar com elles quinta feira que vem, pelas cinco horas.

2.

A senhora A. faz os seus comprimentos à senhora B. e roga-lhe de lhe fazer a honra de vir passar o serão em sua casa terça feira que vem. Haverá jogo de cartas.

3.

O senhor L., vendo-se necessitado a partir para o campo amanhã, pede ao senhor M. de não ter o incommodo de vir á sua casa. O senhor L. folgará muito de receber o senhor M. depois d'amanhã ás horas-que lhe forem commodas.

4.

Ao senhor L., da parte do Senhor B.

Está o dia tão lindo que eu o espero em casa depois do jantar. Passearemos pela tapada, e depois iremos tomar chá no jardim de L., e lá nos divertiremos até á noite. Não se esqueça de vir logo que tiver jantado.

5.

Reposta.

Rogo-lhe de não esperar por mim esta tarde, por que não posso dispôr de mim todo a serão. O portador lhe dirá os motivos que me obrigão a differir para outro dia a satis-facção de o ver. Estou persuadido que Vm. osha de achar justos, e ha de acreditar que sou com profundo respeito.

6.

Ao senhor M. da parte do Senhor T.

Rogo-lhe de ter a bondade mandar-me o livro que lhe emprestei logo que Vm. o tiver lido, porque minha irmão tem grande vontade de o ler em Vm. tendo acabado. He Vm. tão civil que estou certo fará toda a diligencia para me obsequiar.

Queira Vm. aceitar entretanto o testemunho da distincta estima com que sou, etc.

7.

Reposta.

Restituo-lhe o livro que me emprestou, cuja leitura causoume grande satisfacção. Estou certo que tambem o fará á senhora sua irmã; elle he muito divertido, e instructivo para a gente moça, que folga de se instruir.

Cartas de Commercio.

8.

CARTA CIRCULAR.

Senhor

em

Lisboa.

Tomamos a liberdade por em presença e á disposição de VM. a Casa de Negocio, que nesta acabamos de estabelecer.

Meios sufficientes e necessaria practica, adquirida em Escriptorios de primeira reputação, nos poem em estado de cumprir as ordems, de que nossos amigos nos honrarem, á inteira satisfacção delles.

Ainda que intentamos dedicar-nos de preferencia á Commissoens e Expediçoens, não seremos, em convidando as conjuncturas, indispostos á emprezas de propria, como de mutua Conta.

Em quanto a nossa moralidade, darão os Snrs. N & N. cabal informação de nos.

Rogamos tomar nota de nossa Firma e Assignaturas em baixo, e certificar-se do grande respeito, com que somos

De VM.

Veneradores e Criados

A. & B.

9.

Senhores *A. B. & C*ª· em Lisboa.

Londres 1. de Abril.

Reconhecendo a preeminenciä da geralmente preconisada Casa de VMˢ· o temos por nosso primeiro dever levar á presença della o Estabelecimento, que no Circulare junto annunciamos.

Fiados no benigno agazalho da offerta, que de nosso serviço lhes facemos, consideraremos͵nos por extremo ditosos em nos ver favorecidos das prezadissimas ordems de VMˢ as quaes zelaremos de maneira, que mereçamos a continuação dellas; manifestado em todo tempo o nosso grande desejo de͵ promover a utilidade de VMˢ

Na esperanca de favoravel acolhimento dos nossos offerecimentos, confessamos nos

DeVMˢ

addict.ᵐᵒˢ Criados

C. & D.

10.

Senhores *C. & D.* em Londres.

Lisboa 28. de Abril.

Honrados da de nos muito estimada Carta de VMˢ do 1ᵐᵒ do actual mez, tomamos gostosa noticia do seu Estabelecimento, ao qual appetecemos augmento e continuadas prosperidades.

Não deixaremos de utilisar-nos das suas offertas em se apresentando occasião para isso. Por agora não temos com que occupar a VMˢ que a insignificancia de

50 Saccos de Arroz de Santos, e
50 ditos de Cacao de Maranham,

constantes do incluso Conhecimento.

Sendo o Brigue Dido portador destes Saccos, muito bom de vela, o esperamos ao receber desta la a salvo; razão que lhes não encarregamos a Seguro.

Em quanto a venda, se servirão de a fazer pelo estado

daquella terra ao melhor que puderem, avisando nos do suc-
cedido.

Esperando ser por este ensaio animados a ulteriores emprezas ficamos

DeVM^s.

affeiçoados amigos

A. B. & C?

11.

'Senhores *C. & D.* em Londres.

Figueira 10. de Maio.

Tendo eu aos Snr^s. *A. B. & C*? em Lisboa de agrade-
cer o conhecimento da respeitavel Casa de VM^s. tomo a liberdade de consignar á ella as trinta Pipas de Vinho no junto
conhecimento declaradas.

Este Vinho, cuja qualidade he muito boa, rogo vender o
melhor e mais promptamente, que o estado dessa terra o per-
mittir; applicando o producto ao pagamento de hum Saque,
que aos Snr^s. *Richards & C*? em Riga ordeno, que sobre
VM^s. fação; ficando, caso neste pagamento haja excesso contra mim, o reembolço de VM^s ao meu particular cuidado.

O navio Boreas, por quem estes Vinhos vão, intenta sahir dentro de oito dias, e tem alias a fama de bom valeiro.
Com tudo succedendo, que ao receber desta ainda la não
esteja, quizera dever-lhes o favor de mandar segurar estas
trinta Pipas no valor de

Reis 1,200,000 zelando tanto a solidez do Segurador que
a barateza do premio.

Queirão, do que passarem, fazer sciente a este

Seu

sincero Venerador

F. T.

12.

Senhores *A. B. & C*ª em Lisboa.

Londres 30. de Maio.

Foi com inexpressivel gosto que recebemos a Prezadissima de VMˢ de 28. do passado mez, e nella Conhecimento sobre o que pelo Brigue Dido fizerão mercé de consignar-nos.

Este navio, achando-se tres dias antes, que o aviso de VMˢ nos viesse á mão, felizmente surto neste rio; poupou a VMˢ o seguro e entregou nos os cem Saccos bem accondicionados.

Por nos parecer a conjunctura favoravel, tratamos sem demora de sua venda, daqual servimos incluso com a Conta, cujo liquido producto de

£ 150. está a disposição de VMˢ

He a momentanea falta, que actualmente destes generos aqui ha, á qual se devem os preços, que obtivemos e quaes esperamos não deixaró de merecer a approvação de VMˢ

No tudo, de que em diante nos quizerem occupar, achar-nos hão.

Seus
promptos Criados
C. D.

———————

13.

Senhores *A & B*. em Hamburgo.

Porto 27. de Maio.

He por recommendação de meu amigo o Snr. *F. T.* em Figueira, que tomo a confiança de dirigir-me a VM. com a supplica de me mandar em

4 Lastros de Trigo
1   do.   de Centeio
1   do.   de Cevada
½ do.   de Ervilha
½ do.   de Feijão

tudo da melhor qualidade e arrezoado preço.

Estes Grãos desejo receber pelo primeiro navio que dessa á esta, vier, e seguro contra todo risco.

Ao remetter da Conta queirão embolçár-se do emporte, saccando-o sobre mim a trez mezes e ao Cambio mais favoravel, que acharem; na certeza de prompta satisfacção de minha parte.

Na esperança, que este ensaio me animará á continuadas emprezas, sou

De VM^s
sincero Venerador
L. S.

———— —

14.

Senhor *L. S.* em Porto.

Hamburgo 1. de Julho.

Agradecidos ao Snr. *F. T.* em Figueira da muito Prezada da VM. de 27. de Maio. estimamos muito ella nos ter chegado á mão em tempo, que cá ainda estava o navio Mentor. Este navio, no que nos appressamos fazer o embarque dos Grãos de sua ordem, hindo abarrotado com elles partio hontem com favoravel vento.

Emcluso servimos com Conhecimento e Factura, esta ultima de

B.-Mk. 1419. —. no emporte, do que nos prevalecemos, saccando o hoje sobre VM. á 3 mezes, e ao Cambio de 51s com

Reis 445 . 254 cujos pómos debaixo de sua honrosa protecção.

Na esperança de serem estes Grãos tanto na qualidade que no preço á satisfacção de VM. lisonjeamos nos da continuacção das suas apetecidas ordems, em cuja boa execução mostraremos quanto somos

De VM.
zelosos Criados
A. & B.

————

15.

Senhor *T.* em Figueira.

Hamburgo 1. de Agosto.

Favorecidos da Estimad^{ma} de VM. de 10. de Maio damos aos nossos amigos Snr^s *A., B & C^a* em Lisboa as devidas graças de nos terem feito lembrados a VM.; ficando ao nosso cuidado responder dignamente á tam honrosa recommendação.

Em observancia do contendo de sobredita sua Carta fizemos, por ainda não haver noticias do Boreas, o Seguro, a qual
effeituamos ao premio bem modico de $1^1/_2\%$.

Tendo este navio oito dias ao depois chegado e nos en-
tregado as 30 pipas de Vinho em bom estado; cuidamos sem
demora de sua venda, a qual fizemos ao nosso ver de modo,
que VM. não será queixoso della; mormente considerando os
Vinhos desse paiz não serem dos mais procurados nesta praça.

Junto vai a Conta de Venda delles, cujo liquido producto
B.-Mk. 2830. 15. applicaremos ao pagamento do Saque, que
os Snr⁹ *Richards & Cª* em Riga sobre nos tem de fazer.

Do que em diante se passar, lhe daremos prompto aviso
e recommendando nos ao seu ulterior serviço, ficamos

De VM.
attendos Criados
A. & B.

16.

Senhores *A. & B.* em Hamburgo.

Lisboa 15. de Julho.

Com a muito Estimada de VM⁹ de 30. de Maio recebemos Conta de Venda do Arroz e Cacao, que pelo Dido lhes
tinhamos consignado, e contentes do resultado agradecemos
lhes a sua cuidadosa diligencia.

Fiados na mesma ordenamos aos Snr⁹ *K. e Filho* de
Norimberga, que mandem á Casa de seis Caixas de Quin-
calha, e saquem o emporte a 3 mezes de data da Factura
sobre a mesma. Rogamos fazer este pagamento, e enviar nos
os ditos Volumes seguros contra todo risco.

Juntamente queremos dever-lhes a prompta remess de

6 Caixas de Olandas e
4 ditas de Bretanhas

tudo de boa qualidade e justo preço. Ao embolço de huma e
outra cousa lhes servirá, alem do producto do Arroz e Cacao
o que lhes consignaremos logo que chegar o nosso navio Ulysses,
que de Bahia esperamos.

Entre tanto permanecemos

Seus
sinceros Amigos
A. B. & Cª

Senhores *F. T.* em Figueira.

Hamburgo 31. de Agosto.

Confirmando a nossa Precedente d? 1 do actual mez, que servia de capa á Conta de Venda dos seus Vinhos; temos hoje de participar lhe, que os Snr⁹ *Richards & C⁹* em Riga de conta de VM. se prevalecerão sobre nos a 30 dias vista da quantia de

Bco.-Mk. 2730. —. quaes aceitamos e satisfaremos com toda promptidão.

Encontrando se este Saque com o producto dos Vinho ficão segundo a Nota embaixo

Bco.-Mk. 80. 13. em favor e á disposicão de VM.

Para tudo mais que por calhe occorrer, achar nos ha

Seus
promptos Servos
A. & B.

Idiomatic Expressions.

with

Verbs, Adverbs, Prepositions etc.

Andar a pé.	To go on foot.
Andar de pé.	To be unwell.
Andar a cavallo.	To go on horseback.
Andar em coche.	To drive in a carriage.
Andar á vela.	To take a sail.
Andar para diante.	To go forward.
Andar para traz.	To go backward.
Andar a traz de alguem.	To follow some one.
Andar com o tempo.	To go with the times.
Andar perdido.	To go astray.
Andar com honra.	To act honorably.
Andar de esguelha.	To go badly.
Andar de mal para peor.	Out of the frying-pan into the fire.
Com o andar do tempo.	In the course of time.

Andar de galope.	To canter.
Dar um passeio, uma volta.	To take a walk.
Dar a entender.	To give to understand.
Dar fé.	To believe, to credit.
Dar fiado.	To give credit.
Dar á luz.	To publish.
Dar principio.	To begin.
Dar fim.	To end.
Dar os bons dias.	To say good day.
Dar os parabens.	To congratulate.
O relogio dá horas.	The clock strikes.
Dar boa conta de si.	To behave well.
Eu derei conta d'isso.	I will be answerable for it.
Dar em ridicularias.	To become ridiculous.
Dar-se pressa.	To be in a hurry.
Não se lhe dá de morrer.	He does not fear death.
Estar escrevendo.	To be writing.
Estar em pé.	To stand erect.
Estar assentado.	To sit.
Está para chover.	It is going to rain.
Estar em duvida.	To be in doubt.
Estar na cama.	To lie in bed.
Estar com, em, de, saúde.	To be well.
Não esta no meu poder.	It is not in my power.
Estar de posse.	To be in possession.
Fazer esmólas.	To give alms.
Faz frio.	It is cold.
Faz lua.	The moon shines.
Não faço caso delle.	I do not care for him.
Fazer uma festa.	To give a party.
Fazer lugar.	To make room.
Ter que fazer.	To have to do.
Fazer um discurso.	To make a speech.
Fazer uma aposta.	To lay a wager.
Faz hoje oito dias.	It is a week to-day.
Fazer o possivel.	To do one's utmost.
Não henho que fazer com isso.	I have nothing to do with it.
Fazer-se velho.	To become old.
Fazer-se feio.	To become ugly.
Faz-se tarde.	It is getting late.
Ter razão.	To be in the right.
Não ter razão.	To be in the wrong.

Ter ciumes.	To be jealous.
Que quer dizer isto?	What is the meaning of it?
Isto quer dizer, que ...	It means that ...
Ha alguma cousa de novo?	Is there any news?
Ha muito tempo.	It is a long time ago.
Ha um anno.	It is a year ago.
Hir por diante.	To go forward.
Eilo lá vai	There he goes.
Hir para traz.	To go back.
Hir buscar.	To fetch.
Nada se vai mais depressa que o tempo.	Nothing passes quicker than time.
Vai-se fazendo tarde.	It becomes late.
Não tenho medo.	I have no fear.
Não mais.	Not more.
Ainda não.	Not yet.
Não o farei.	I shall not do it.
Não uuuito depois.	Not long after.
Queres fazer isso ou não?	Will you do it or not?
Um diz sim, e outro não.	One says yes, the other no.
Não he bom nem máo.	It is neither good nor bad.
Elle ainda não veio.	He has not yet come.
Até onde?	How far?
Até Roma.	To Rome.
Até quando?	How long?
Até que eu vivo.	As long as I live.
Como assim?	How so?
Como! não quereis vir?	What! you will not come?
Dez libras quando muito.	At utmost ten pounds.
Dez libras quando menos.	At least ten pounds.
Dizei muito embora o que quizerdes.	You may say what you like.
Assim he?	Is it so?
Assim seja.	Be it so.
Basta assim por agora.	It is enough for the present.
Andar a passos lentes.	To go very slowly.
A' direita.	To the right.
A' esquerda.	To the left.
Vir de França.	To come from France.
Venho da casa da Senhora N.	I come from Mrs. N.
De madrugada.	Early in the morning.
De noite.	By night.

De dia.	By day.
De verão.	In summer.
Perto de oito horas.	Towards eight o'clock.
Junto á cidade.	Near the town.
Sobre a mesa	Upon the table.
Sobre a noite.	Towards night.
Sobre todas as cousas.	Before all things.
Duas vezes no dia.	Twice a day.
Na rua.	On the street.
Em todo o tempo.	At all times.
Em premio.	For reward.
Para que he isto?	What is that for?
Para onde?	Where to?
Para que fim?	For what purpose?
Palavra por palavra.	Word for word.
Vai por vinho.	Fetch wine.
De muito atraz.	Far back.
Fazer passo atraz.	To take a step backwards.
Alguns dias atraz.	A few days ago.

LIST OF PORTUGUESE BOOKS

published and imported by
FRANZ THIMM
European and Oriental Bookseller.

24 Brook Street, Grosvenor Square, London,
A well assorted Stock of the

German, French, Italian, Spanish, Swedish, Danish, Dutch, Russian,
as well as **Oriental Languages** is always on hand.

Cabano's Portuguese Grammar, with Exercises. A new practical and easy Method. 3rd Edit. 8vo. Cloth. 1869.	0	4	0
Monteiro's Portuguese and English Idiomatic Dialogues.	0	2	6
Vieyra's Portuguese and English Dictionary. 12m. roan.	0	10	0

2. With French

Constancio. Grammaire Portugaise	0	3	0
Dialogues, Portugais-français 12o	0	2	6
Fonseca, Dictionaire portugais français 2 vols. 8⁰ sewed.	0	18	0

3. With German

Ollendorf's Portugiesische Grammatik	0	6	0
— key to ditto	0	2	0
Bösche's Portugiesische Sprachlehre. 1853.	0	5	6
— Portugiesisch-deutsche Gespräche.	0	3	6
— Portugiesisch-deutsches Wörterbuch. 2 vols. 8vo.	0	18	0
Wollheim, Portugiesisches Handwörterbuch. 12mo. . .	0	8	0

Portuguese Literature.

Camões, Os Lusiadas. Poemo epico. ed. Fonseca. 8vo. 1846.	0	9	0
— ditto. 12mo.	0	3	6
Correspondencia Commercial, (Portuguese & French) 1857	0	4	0
Collecção de autores portuguezes vol. I. Dias, G. Cantos. 2 vols. 1860.	7	0	
Constancio, Historia de Brasil (Portuguese). 2 vols. 8vo.	0	12	0
Darosta, Historia de Portugal (Portuguese). 3 vols. 12mo.	0	10	6
Fenelon, Aventuras de Telemaco	0	4	0
Fonseca, Prosas Selectas, ou escolha dos melhores logares dos auctores portuguezes. 1855.	0	4	6

Printed by J. B. Hirschfeld at Leipsic.

LIST OF THE BEST BOOKS

for the Study of Foreign Languages
published by
FRANZ THIMM,
Foreign Bookseller and Publisher,
24 Brook Street, Grosvenor Square, London W.

Post Office Orders to be made payable at Vere Street

FRANZ THIMM'S
Series of
EUROPEAN, ORIENTAL AND CLASSICAL GRAMMARS
after an easy and practical Method, with Exercises, Reading-Lessons and
Dialogues.

All uniform in size 8vo. and neatly bound in Cloth.	£	s.	d.
GERMAN GRAMMAR by Meissner. 10th Ed. 1867 .	0	3	6
„ Key to ditto sewed	0	1	0
FRENCH GRAMMAR by Ahn. 8th Ed. 1867 . .	0	3	6
„ Key to ditto sewed	0	1	0
ITALIAN GRAMMAR by Marchetti. 4th Ed. 1863 .	0	4	0
„ Key to ditto sewed	0	1	0
SPANISH GRAMMAR by Salvo. 2nd Ed. 1862 . .	0	4	0
„ Key to ditto sewed	0	1	0
PORTUGUESE GRAMMAR by Cabano. 2nd Ed. 1860	0	4	0
SWEDISH GRAMMAR by Lenström. 2nd Ed. 1861	0	4	0
DANISH GRAMMAR by Lund. 2nd Ed. 1860 . .	0	4	0
„ Key to ditto sewed	0	1	6
DUTCH GRAMMAR by Ahn. 2nd Ed. 1860 . . .	0	4	0
HEBREW GRAMMAR by Herxheimer. 1862 . . .	0	4	0
„ Key to ditto sewed	0	2	0
LATIN GRAMMAR by Seidenstücker. 2nd Ed. 1862	0	3	0
„ Key to ditto.	0	1	6
RUSSIAN GRAMMAR by J. Alexandrow. 1867 . .	0	4	0
MODERN GREEK GRAMMAR by A. Vlachos. 1867	0	4	0
ICELANDIC GRAMMAR by Rask	0	4	0

Franz Thimm's
Series of European Grammars
combine Theory with Practice, and follow the ideas which eminent men have
adopted, as to the clearest and most rational method of teaching languages.

The celebrated philosopher *Leibnitz* remarked *"my opinion with regard
to grammar is this, most is learned by use — the rules must be added for
finish"* and the learned philologist *Facciolati* observes, *I am indebted to the
classical authors for every thing I know, to the grammarians I owe nothing."*

SEIDENSTÜCKER, was the first who in 1811 introduced this new Method
for the Latin, Greek and French languages, and to him belongs in justi[ce]
the merit, of having introduced a rational system of tuition. Ahn who [m]
use of this method long after in 1834, acknowledges in his Preface, Se[i]

stücker as the originator of the System. But there was an essential point
omitted even in these books. It was, that the

      "grammatical form should *precede* the Exercises, so that the learner
      "should at once be made acquainted with the grammatical structure
      "of the foreign language, without which, he could never attain a
      "thorough knowledge of it".

This then is the principle which has been followed in "FRANZ THIMM's
Series of European Grammars" and which gives it a distinct feature of
progress over the former systems pursued.

The prevalent idea in these grammars is that of teaching a language
easily and pleasantly, of adapting it to every capacity, of removing all unnecessary difficulties and at the same time of imparting the necessary grammatical knowledge.

In this respect therefore

"Franz Thimm's Series of Grammars"

is not only original, but extending the new Method to all the languages of
Europe, it is unique.

Franz Thimm's
NEW SERIES OF FOREIGN DIALOGUES,

On an entirely new and practical plan, calculated to insure a rapid
acquisition of Foreign Languages. 12mo. Cloth.

				£	s.	d.
GERMAN	and ENGLISH Dialogues,		by Meissner.	0	2	6
FRENCH	„	„	„	by Dudevant.	0	2	6
ITALIAN	„	„	„	by Marchetti.	0	2	6
SPANISH	„	„	„	by Salvo.	0	2	6
PORTUGUESE	„	„	„	by Monteiro.	0	2	6
SWEDISH	„	„	„	by Lenström.	0	2	6
DANISH	„	„	„	by Lund.	0	2	6
DUTCH	„	„	„	by Harlen.	0	2	6

Turkish, Russian, English and French Vocabulary for Travellers in the East. 0 2 6

A correct and fluent conversation will soon be obtained by the use of
these Dialogues for they contain nothing but important matter. The words
generally in use, the easy colloquial phrases and the idiomatic expressions
of the language, which form the essence of correct conversation, have been
carefully arranged, so as to make these Dialogues really useful.

Published by Mr. FRANZ THIMM, Foreign Publisher, 24 Brook Street,
Grosvenor Square, London.

Dialogues in 3 Languages.

FRANZ THIMM'S
TRAVELLER'S PRACTICAL MANUAL
OF CONVERSATION IN THREE LANGUAGES
ENGLISH, GERMAN AND FRENCH.
16°. boards. — 2 *s.*

TRAVELLER'S PRACTICAL MANUAL
OF CONVERSATION IN FOUR LANGUAGES
ENGLISH, GERMAN, FRENCH AND ITALIAN.
16°. boards. — 3 *s.* 6 *d.*
"*Useful for travellers or for the study of comparative languages.*"

Just published

in a wrapper 8vo. "one Shilling" each

FRANZ THIMM'S

FRENCH SELF-TAUGHT,
GERMAN SELF-TAUGHT,
ITALIAN SELF-TAUGHT,
SPANISH SELF-TAUGHT,

A new System on the most simple principles for self-tuition, with the complete english pronunciation of every word, table of coins etc. 8vo. Price "one Shilling" sewed.

Very practical and useful introductory - treatises for self-tuition with the correct pronunciation of these languages.

The most approved Books for the tuition of Foreign Languages.
German Language.

I. For the Nursery.

	£	s.	d.
CHILD'S GERMAN BOOK by Hahn. 3rd Ed. 12mo. Cl.	0	3	0

"An excellent and easy Book for Children."

SCHMIDT, CH., One Hundred German Tales, with english notes by Mathias. 5th Ed. 8vo. 1866. Cloth. ... 0 2 0

"Simple moral tales written in an easy german style, the "very best book for beginners."

HAHN'S Interlinear German Reading Book, for self-tuition. (Hamiltonian Method.) 8vo. 1857. Cloth. 0 2 6

THE FIRST BOOK OF GERMAN POETRY. Deutsche Gedichte für den ersten Unterricht, ausgewählt von F. Geissler. 12mo. 1857. Cloth.. . . . . . 0 2 6

"Containing German Nursery Rhymes, Fables, and Poems "of an easy verse and construction, gradually rising to and in-"cluding the minor poems of Schiller, Goethe and Uhland. All "selected to be learnt by heart."

LESSING'S Fabeln (Prose and Verse) with english notes by Hill. 12mo. 1859. boards. 0 1 6

"Of a classic simplicity. Text book for Government "Examinations."

GERMAN SELF-TAUGHT, with complete pronunciation of every word. 8vo. sewed 0 1 0

II. For the Class Room.

MEISSNER, M., A new practical and easy method of learning the German Language. Tenth corrected Edition. 1867. 8vo. Cloth.. . . . . . 0 3 6

"This Grammar, which has at once embraced and super-"ceeded all former systems, is one of the most valuable german "Grammars published — it is not only an easy book for be-"ginners, but also a desirable class book for progressive study "Professors pronounce it the "best german Grammar ever "published."

" Key to ditto. sewed. 0 1 0

JULIUS, German Writing Copies (Deutsche Vorschriften.) 3rd Ed. oblong. 8vo. 1863. sewed . . . 0 1 8

"These Copyslips are simple and graceful in form, they "are methodical and the proper modern handwriting."

FRANZ THIMM'S GERMAN COPY BOOK. A new and
complete Method, imparting a modern and elegant
form of German Handwriting. 4to. 0 1 6
"A perfect Method of german writing very useful for Schools
"and Classes."

HAHN'S GERMAN TALES AND STORIES; including
Hauff's kalte Herz — Schmidt's Täubchen — Auer-
bach, des Waldschützen Sohn, for progressive reading
with english notes. 8vo. 1857. Cloth . . . 0 3 6

CAROVE'S MÄRCHEN OHNE ENDE (the story without
an end) with english notes by Mathias. 16mo.
Cloth gilt edged 0 2 0
"Nowhere will you find the book of nature more freshly and
"beautifully opened, than in Carové's 'Märchen ohne Ende' of its
"kind one of the best that was ever written."
                    Quarterly Review January 1867.

SCHMIDT'S German Plays, adapted for School-Reading
with english notes by A. E. Hill. 8vo. Cloth . 0 5 0
              or separately:
Part I. Die Erdbeeren — Der kleine Kaminfeger 0 1 6
  - II. Der Blumenkranz — Der Eeierdieb . . 0 1 6
  - III. Emma oder die kindliche Liebe . . . 0 1 6
"Adapted for children, and may easily be acted."

KOTZEBUE'S Deutsche Kleinstädter, with notes by
Meissner. 8vo. 0 2 0

KOTZEBUE'S Pagenstreiche, with notes by Meissner. 8. 0 2 0
"The text of these two Comedies has been altered in this
"edition, so as to adapt them for Ladies and Schools. Only
"these Editions by "Meissner" can be safely used."

MEISSNER'S German and English Idiomatic Phrases and
Dialogues. 4th Ed. 12mo. Cloth. 1867. . . 0 2 6
"This Dialogue and Phrasebook only contains useful matter,
"such as will give great facility of expression in speaking the
"language. Very useful for Travellers."

III. For the Senior Class.

THIMM, F., the Literature of Germany from its earliest
Period to the present time. Historically deve-
loped. 2nd Ed. illustrated, fscap. 8vo. Cloth. 1866. 0 5 0
"Among publications of a superior kind, fitted to give an
"excellent sketch of the rise and progress of German literature,
"we are acquainted with no work so well adapted as Mr. Thimm's,
"of which a new edition has just appeared. The characters of
"the leading writers are ably and graphically depicted, and their
"chief works enumerated."
                    Oxford Journal. 17 March 1866.

THIEME'S German Dictionary, publ. by FRANZ THIMM. Cl. 0 7 0

THIEME'S Critical German and English and English
and German Dictionary. imp. 8. bound. 1866 0 12 0
"These two, are the best german and english Dictionaries,
"that can be placed into the hands of the german Scholar. Its
"advantages are numerous. "The accent is given, which facilitates

"the german Pronunciation — to the substantive are added the
"Gender, the genitive, dative and the termination of the plural —
"to the Adjectives are added the irregular comparative forms —
"and to the irregular Verbs all irregularities are added. — The
"print of the Dictionaries is beautiful and the price very low."

MEISSNER. The German Exercise Book, being a
Collection of Exercises intended as a supplement
to every German Grammar, or as a necessary
assistant for German Practice and Self-Tuition.
8vo. Cloth. 1857 . . . . 0 2 6
   ,,   A key to   ditto. 8vo. sewed. 1858 . 0 2 0
"Progressive Exercises, for writing more extended composi-
"tions, tales, letters, historical prose" etc.

GEISSLER. Die schönsten deutschen Balladen und Gedichte. (Collection of the most beautiful German
Ballads and Poems. Goethe, Schiller, Bürger, Uhland,
Heine, Freiligrath etc. etc. Herausgegeben von
Geissler. 2nd Ed., illustrated with the heads of
the chief poets. 8vo. Cloth neat 0 5 0
"This is one of the most beautiful collections of german
"poems published, it gives the essence of all that is grand and
"distinguished in german poetry, and therefore of particular
"value to the student."

COLLECTION of the most esteemed Tales and Novels of
Germany. (Klassischer Novellenkranz.)
"These novels and tales are adapted for Ladies
and Class Readings. vol. I. 8vo. Cloth . . 0 6 0
      ,,   ,,   vol. II. 0 7 0
  1. Zschokke's Abenteuer der Neujahrsnacht, sewed 2nd Ed. 0 1 6
  2. Hauff's Othello 0 1 6
  3. Varnhagen's Sterner und Psitticher 0 1 6
  4. Hoffmann's Fräulein Scuderi, 2nd Edit. 0 1 6
  5. Zschokke, der todte Gast 0 2 0
  6. Kinkel's Hauskrieg 0 1 0
  7. Stifter's Hochwald 0 2 0
  8. Zschokke's Fürstenblick 0 1 6
  Part. 5 to 8 forms the 2nd Volume Cloth 0 7 0
  Part 9 Zschokke's Loch im Aermel 0 1 6

ZSCHOKKE'S Vier Erzählungen. Cloth 0 7 0
"Nothing is more difficult than to recommend to German
"Scholars a good volume of elegant prose, which will make them
"acquainted with the best authors and also tend to unite amuse-
"ment with instruction. This Collection presents the Reader with
"nine Masterpieces' elegant and amusing tales by excel-
"lent writers and also with such as may safely be placed
"in the hands of every one without danger; in consequence
"slight alterations of text have been deemed necessary, so as to
"make these tales suitable for young ladies and for classes."

FRANCK'S Deutscher Briefsteller. (German Letter- 0 3 6
writer.) 8vo. Cloth. . . . .
"This collection not only facilitates the composition of ger-
"man letters, but serves the scholar as a book of study and as a
"model of german prose composition, for it contains a collec-
"tion of letters by classical german authors."

THIMM'S
CLASSICAL GERMAN DRAMAS.

	£	s.	d.
SCHILLER'S Neffe als Onkel, with english Notes by M. Meissner. 12mo. 1866. boards	0	1	6

"The text has been slightly modified so as to give this Edi-
"tion a 'distinct character' as a Class Book."

SCHILLER'S Wilhelm Tell, with english notes by M. Meissner. 12mo. 1859	0	2	0

GOETHE'S EGMONT, with english notes by O. v. Wegnern. 12mo. 1863	0	2	0

"The notes to these celebrated Dramas are historical, gram-
"matical and explanatory, and facilitate the reading and appre-
"ciation of these classical pieces."

French Language.
I. Step.

THE CHILD'S FRENCH BOOK by Hahn. Cloth	0	3	0

"This is the first book for the nursery."

AHN'S French Class Book for Beginners, being the first Course of the French Method adapted from the german original and improved by Dudevant. 4th Edition. 1862	0	1	6

"This remarkable book was published first in Germany and
"has now reached the 150th Edition!"

FRENCH SELF-TAUGHT, A new system, on the most simple principles for self-tuition, with the complete english pronunciation of every word	0	1	0

POÉSIES DE L'ENFANCE, chosies par François Louis. (French Poetry for Children.) 12mo. 1859. boards	0	2	0

"This collection has been made with great care, giving easy
"and short pieces such as are rarely found in similar collections
"and are adapted for the youngest children."

II. Step.

FRENCH GRAMMAR by Ahn. "Author's eighth Edition." 8vo. Cloth. 1867	0	3	6
Key to ditto. 1858	0	1	0

"This is one of the most remarkable school books ever pub-
"lished for the french language."

FRENCH READER compiled after Ahn and other Readers by Dudevant. With English Notes. 8vo. Cloth.	0	1	6

It contains: I. Detached sentences, Substantives, Adjectives
Pronouns, Verbs, Particles. II. Anecdotes. III Short pieces from
Natural history. IV. Fables. V. Tales. VI. Descriptive Prose.

DUDEVANT'S French and English Idiomatic Phrases and Dialogues; indispensable for a rapid acquisition of the French Language. 12mo. 1856. Cloth	0	2	6

SPIER'S French and English and English and French Dictionaries. 2 Vol. 8vo. 1854. Cloth	1	1	0
„ ditto. ditto. abridged 12mo.	0	7	6

BARRET'S French and English pocket Dictionary. 24. Cloth 1855.	0	4	6

The Princess Alexandra and the Royal House of
Denmark. A Genealogy; giving an account of Danish history from the Sea-Kings-down to the family
of the Princess of Wales. 12mo. 1863 . . . . . 0 1 0

Swedish Language.

	£	s.	d.
LENSTRÖM'S Swedish Grammar. 2nd Ed. 8vo. Cl. 1861	0	4	0
„ Swedish and Engl. Dialogues. 12mo. 1857	0	2	6
„ Svensk Loesebog i prosa og poesi. 8. 1843	0	6	0
„ Sveriges Litteratur Historia. 8vo. 1841	0	6	0
TEGNER'S Frithiofs-Saga. 12mo	0	2	6
Swedish and English Dictionary. 12mo. Cloth. 1857	0	5	0

Dutch Language.

	£	s.	d.
AHN'S Dutch Grammar. 2nd. Ed. 1860. 8vo. Cloth	0	4	0
HARLEN'S Dutch and Engl. Dialogues. 12mo. Cl. 1858	0	2	6
Dutch and English Dictionary. 12mo. Cloth	0	5	0

Russian and Turkish Languages.

	£	s.	d.
Russian, Turkish, French and English Vocabulary for Travellers in the East. 2nd Ed. 12mo. Cl. 1858	0	2	6
ALEXANDROW'S Russian Grammar. 8vo. 1867. Cloth	0	4	0
Russian and English Dictionary. 12mo. Cloth . . .	0	5	0

Modern Greek Language.

	£	s.	d.
VLACHO'S Modern Greek Grammar, 8vo. 1867. Cloth	0	4	0
BYZANTIUS Dictionnaire grec-franç. et fr.-gr. imp. 8vo.	1	5	0
DEHÈQUE, Dictionnaire grec moderne française. 12mo.	0	8	0

Commercial Correspondences.

GERMAN AND ENGLISH, Commercial Correspondence ⎫
FRENCH AND ENGLISH   ditto   by Dudevant ⎪
ITALIAN AND ENGLISH   ditto   by Marchetti ⎬ in the press.
SPANISH AND ENGLISH   ditto   by Salvo ⎭

	£	s.	d.
FLÜGEL'S Triglotte, oder kaufmännisches Wörterbuch. Deutsch, Englisch, Französisch. 8vo.	0	14	0
RHODE'S praktisches Handbuch der Handels-Correspondenz deutsch, französisch, englisch und italienisch. 8vo. Cl.	0	10	6
MANITIUS, der kaufmännische Correspondent deutsch, englisch, französisch, italienisch und spanisch . .	0	6	0
SCHULTEN, deutsche, holländische, französische und englische Handels-Correspondenz. 8 vo.	0	7	0
LEIPZIGER Handels-Correspondent	0	5	0
FORT, kaufmännische Correspondenz	0	7	0
KEEGAN'S kaufmännische Phraseologie in französischer *und englischer* Sprache	0	2	6

SHAKSPEARIANA
from 1564 to 1864.
An account of the Shakspearian Literature
of
England, Germany and France
during three Centuries
with Bibliographical Introductions,
by
Franz Thimm.
London 1865. 8°. Cloth. 4 *s.*

"The author has laid the student of Shakspearian literature under deep
"obligations. That literature is now of itself an important and distinctive
"branch of study. Innumerable essays, criticisms, commentaries, expositions,
"and lectures upon Shakespeare have been published in England, Germany
"and France. Their titles, authors' names, and dates of appearance have
"been collected together by Mr. Thimm, and arranged in alphabetical order.
"Prefixed to each list is an historical account of the progress of Shakspea-
"rian criticism in the three countries, which instructively shows the growth
"of the appreciation of the exhaustless dramas. The book is both valuable
"as a reference, and as a study of the advance in the English and Conti-
"nental estimation of Shakspeare. It is the fullest compilation of the kind
"we have; Bohn's edition of Lowndes has hitherto been the most complete
"record on the subject; but to the works there enumerated Mr. Thimm has
"added the titles of at least one hundred and seventy more books in the
"English, and nearly three hundred in the German and French Department.
"Mr. Thimm's is therefore the most perfect collection of Shakspeariana."

It has been his "endeavour to place before the lovers of the great dra-
matistes" an elaborate Catalogue of what the Times calls the "Shakspeare
Library" and he has succeeded in accomplishing his object.

Shrewsbury Observer. 1865.

From the Preface.

The first "Shakspeariana" by Wilson, published in 1827 was too imperfect to be of much use.

Mr. Halliwell's, which appeared in 1841, is very useful for the various
early editions of Shakspeare's works; but for so great a student of the dramatist and his history, his collection of Commentaries and essays (which
only extends to 233 numbers) is singularly imperfect. Sillig's Shakspeare
Literatur bis Mitte 1854 was decidedly the most perfect production of its
kind, which had hitherto seen the light.

Nevertheless I could not relinquish the idea of publishing my own
Collectanea; for notonly were my materials and the labour expended upon
them considerable (the subject has occupied me for more than 12 years)
but it was moreover a part of my plan to classify the productions of England, France and Germany, in a manner as yet unattempted. Halliwell had
only 26 additions to Wilson, I had over 600 more than Sillig, enough in
themselves to constitute quite a new work. The latest addition to Shakspearian literature has appeared in the new edition of "Lowndes-Manuel" by
Mr. Henry Bohn, and constitutes a "Shakspeariana" of which I cannot but
speak in the very highest terms. And yet it will be found, on comparison,
that I have at least 120 additional references in the English, and nearly
300 in the German and French departments.

"Southey said, when Isaac Reed's contribution appeared, Comments
"upon Shakspeare keep pace with the National Debt: yet I should like to
"see his book and would buy it, if I could. Of course; and a costly store
"is obtained by such continual additions"

The complete Catalogue, as far as it is possible for a Bibliographer to
give, of this Shakespeare "Library" it has been my endeavour to place before the lovers of the great dramatist.